POENA CULLEI

A NOVEL

BRITO KODENKANDATH

ISBN 979-888591483-3

Contents

Preface

The thoughts and opinions expressed in this book are those
of the author's alone.
The characters and the situations in this novel are fictional.
Text copyright © 2021 Brito Kodenkandath
E-mail: britoofficial1207@gmail.com
IG: @iam_bk12
<u>Editor</u>
Ashlyn K Joy
Email: ashlyn.joygeorge@gmail.com
IG: @ashlyn.joy
<u>Cover</u>
Jibin Somachandran
IG: @jibinartist

In Loving Memory Of Mohinder Master

PREFACE

Acknowledgements

Hello everyone,

I thank all of you, who contributed to this story to finish it on time.

The story thread was given by my roommate, colleague, and moreover, my friend Rinto Puthurkara helped me a lot throughout the development of the story.

Thank Jibin and Lijin bro for gifting me a wonderful cover image. My doubts were cleared by my unexpected friend Aishwarya(Al Lawyer) thank you.

I thank Editor Ashlyn K Joy, who patiently edited and made my novel readable for you.

Other friends generously gave their time for my story and helped me improvise the novel.

Time for developing this story was a blessing of Covid-19.

I thank my family, friends, colleagues, social media and the internet for great support.

Thanks to all......

Brito Kodenkandath.

CHAPTER ONE

Bombay District court, rumbling with footsteps of reporters and police. Reporters are loudly making live telecasts from every other corner.

'Today is the first trial of Mumbai rape case, all are waiting for the arrival of five suspects who raped her brutally and forced her to end her own life' said one of the reporters looking towards the camera with a straight face.

'Van is approaching the court, clear the area, Over...Over...' one of the wireless phones echoed.

The police troops assembled ahead of the speeding police van with their lathi and took their positions. An old blue van approached the entrance. All reporters started running towards it.

The van stopped in front of the court entrance and police came near the van and blocked all the people to make way for the five suspects to get inside the court.

The doors opened and the handcuffed five young teenagers got out of the van wearing black head covers.

The reporters started throwing questions at the suspects, but nobody gave any reply. Police pushed the crowd out and made way for the suspects.

Somehow police managed to get them inside the court. Just as they entered, the reporters started their live telecasting about the five suspects.

'Here comes the criminal lawyer Johnson Xavier who is

defending the five teenagers, will he save these rapists too?' said one lady reporter looking at the camera.

A black BMW approached slowly to the entrance of the court and stopped at the entrance. The reporters again rushed towards the vehicle and positioned themselves for their sharp questions.

The back door opened and a feet with pure black well polished shoe came out and touched the ground.

A perfectly dressed gentleman with a glossy black suit and black sunglasses came out of the car.

He looked dashing and he was carrying the Lawyer's gown on his left hand.

'Sir, are you confident in this case?' asked one reporter curiously.

'Yes of course, this case will also be closed by my victory' said the criminal lawyer and proudly moved towards court.

Advocate Johnson Xavier was inside the courtroom filled with the public along with his stunning female assistants and took his seat.

One of his assistants handed over a file to him which carried the case details.

An old but confident looking person wearing black with frameless spectacles comes through the door behind the stage.

All the people inside the court including lawyers stood up. Judge took his seat and all sat down.

'Session case number one thousand two hundred seven bar two thousand seventeen' shouted the clerk.

'My lord, I need your permission to cross examine the witness number one' said Advocate Johnson

'Permission granted' judge said.

'Witness number one Miss. Zoya' her name echoed inside the court.

Miss Zoya came to the front and walked towards the witness box facing the five suspects on opposite suspect box.

'Miss. Zoya, what was the relationship between the victim and these boys' lawyer asked looking into Zoya's eyes.

Zoya's face became pale, she glanced at the suspects opposite to her and started to speak.

'They both are my classmates, they are friends'. Zoya said.

'Did she have a good time with these people in college?' Johnson asked his voice changed.

All people inside the court had their eyes fixated on Zoya for the reply. Their faces expressed curiosity.

'Yes, she was always with them happily and she really enjoyed their company' Zoya said in a shaking voice.

The court fell into sudden silence.

'My lord, please note this important point disclosed by the main witness' Johnson said facing the judge and continued.

'Zoya, have you seen anything unusual in their friendship?'

Zoya's face became red. She took a deep breath and gave a glance towards the crowd.

'Yes sir, I have noticed several times that she was taking advantage of these boys, somewhat like friends with benefits' Zoya said this and looked down and closed her eyes.

'My lord, Miss Zoya told that she was enjoying their company and also took sexual advantage of these boys' Johnson said and got back to his seat.

Prosecutor stood up with rage and looked at Johnson and turned towards the judge.

'Lord, I humbly request you to grant permission to examine the Autopsy reports of Dr Kim, along with Dr Kim himself' the prosecutor said.

'You may proceed' the judge said.

'Dr. Kim, Forensic department' clerk called out loudly.

A Black thick spectacled man came slowly towards the witness box. The clerk handed over the autopsy report to the judge.

'Dr. Kim, what is your report on the Autopsy?' prosecutor queried.

'Sir, the body was clean, no marks were present on the body. It was not a raped body, it was young and tender' Dr. Kim said.

Gasping noises surrounded the court. All the evidence against the five suspects were vanishing one by one.

Advocate Johnson stood up quickly.

'My lord, please note this point, it was not a rape, she was clearly enjoying all these activities, then how can we relate her suicide to these innocent teenagers' Advocate Johnson said.

'Mr. Prosecutor, anything to add' the judge asked.

'No, sir' Prosecutor said.

Judge took the wooden hammer from his table and gently hit the wooden tablet twice.

'The judgement of this case has been postponed to October twenty six, two thousand seventeen.'

Judge got up from his seat and left the room.

All the people inside, went out through the six doors of the court with a hopeless face.

One man was still sitting inside the court weeping.

Advocate Johnson took the compliments from the other advocates inside the court and took his files, handed it over to his assistants and walked towards the exit.

Suddenly, the man who was weeping walked towards the lawyer, stood in front and blocked him.

'You will pay for this, you took away my belief in justice' the old man said.

'Truth will always win' Johnson said arrogantly with a smirk on his face.

'I will kill you, you killed my daughter numerous times here' the old man said strongly with rage in his eyes.

Johnson got a little terrified and walked out of the court with his assistants.

A big mob came rushing to the lawyer with lots of questions.

'No comments' Johnson blurted out and moved towards his black BMW.

He entered his car and closed the door.

BMW cruised out of the gate.

'Do you feel anything wrong in what I'm doing?' Johnson asked his assistant inside the car.

'It's our duty, but still humanity' she said.

'Hmm' said Johnson.

He reached his mansion.

He slowed down near a huge gate with a large fence through which emerged a wide driveway leading to a gigantic mansion all in white. The whole premise of the mansion was secured with CCTV.

He stepped out of his car and entered his mansion to freshen up after the long and stressful day. His driver approached him and said.

'Sir, parents of the five are here'

'Tell them to sit in my office' Johnson said.

Johnson wiped his face with a white towel and removed his Black suit and hung it on the stand and went towards his office.

'Good afternoon, all happy' Johnson said to parents with a smiling face.

All of them stood up and folded their hands like they were in a temple.

'Sit...sit...' Johnson said.

'We are very thankful to you sir' one of the parents said.

'I see all are happy, so it's time to make me happy' Johnson said in a silly tone.

'Yes sir' another parent said.

'Hmm good, 5 Cr' Johnson said.

'What sir?' one parent asked in disbelief.

'Per head one crore that I saved from the rope' Johnson said.

All the faces struck pale. They looked at each other.

'Ok sir, we will pay you' one of the parents said smoothly.

'Good fathers, God! Please make many more sons and fathers like this, so I can be a multi-millionaire faster' Johnson said jokingly looking towards them and laughed.

CHAPTER TWO

New York City.

It was a casual Saturday night; a huge party was going on in a crowded nightclub. Laser lights among many other features made up for a great ambience, everyone was in a great mood jazzed up in dance, alcohol and loud music.

A man was wearing a leather jacket dancing in front of the DJ podium with a bunch of hot girls. He was holding a glass of Vodka in his left hand and the other hand was on the waist of a white blonde girl.

After some time he moved into a corner of the club through the darkness with the blonde girl.

'You are so hot…' a young man said with a bit of darkness in his eyes.

She giggled and looked into his eyes.

They came closer and started locking their lips. His hands started moving rapidly behind her and he pressed hard on her butt.

She suddenly gasped and opened her eyes.

'You naughty' she said and giggled.

They laughed and again continued kissing.

Few moments later, he stopped kissing and took his mobile from his jeans' pocket, which was ringing. He turned away from the girl and took the call.

He didn't say a word during the call, and heard everything from the other side.

'I have to go' he said and gave a kiss on her cheek and moved towards the exit.

He walked in a hurry through the dancing floor full of people and out of the club. Two big men with black suits followed him to the car parked in front of the club.

A glossy black Lamborghini Huracan with its front LED lamp on parked in front of nightclub. A perfect badass New York affluent life combination.

Reghu Jadhav, A successful young business man in New York City. He came from a rich Jadhav family in Mumbai. His father Mr. Dhamodhar Jadhav was a big shot, who has various businesses across India. Reghu's grandfather Raja Jadhav was a Judge of Mumbai high court, who was now enjoying his retired life by a little activism and yoga.

#

A beautiful contemporary house situated in south Mumbai. A silver grey Audi A8 was parked in the garage. Very beautifully designed interiors with a Crystal chandelier hanging from the centre of the visitor's room. Heavily worked wooden doors.

In the living room and an old man watching TV, Raja Jadhav, Reghu's grandpa.

'Breaking News, famous criminal lawyer Johnson Xavier found dead near Seawoods Local train station' news reporter on TV said.

The old man got up, shocked.

'Dhamodhar, Dhamodhar' Raja called out loudly.

'Yes pa' a sound came from upstairs.

'Come down, look at this' the old man said, freaking out.

Dhamodhar Jadhav, Reghu's father, came down through the broad curved staircase.

'What pa?' Dhamodhar asked.

'Johnson is dead' grandpa said.

Dhamodhar became speechless.

'What? What happened?' Dhamodhar asked in shock looking towards the TV.

'It's a murder, the body was inside a sack and it was thrown in the canal' grandpa explained after seeing the visuals from TV.

'Who did it?' Dhamodhar asked, his voice whimpering.

'Anyone! Criminal who he saved or the victims' grandpa said with a low voice.

'Need to inform Reghu, how will he take his death?' Dhamodhar said.

'Dad' Reghu entered the house. His eyes were red and voice shattered.

'Reghu you came?' Dhamodhar exclaimed in surprise.

'Who did it dad? Who's responsible for this?' Reghu asked desperately.

'Don't know son' Dhamodhar said in pain.

Reghu sat on the couch and covered his face in his palms.

'Son, we can find out who did this and finish him' Dhamodhar said.

'No, we have the system to punish' Grandpa said.

'I need to leave' Reghu said and dashed out.

#

An old cemetery with white painted graves covered with green grass. A few people walked through the green grass towards a corner of the cemetery.

A priest in white gown with a silver holy cross in his hands, stood near the body of Johnson. People were continuously coming near the grave.

Reghu came for the funeral of Adv. Johnson, he was wearing a black suit with black tie just like most people

'Holy be to the father and to the son and to the Holy Spirit' the priest said.

'Amen' people said.

'You can have the last kisses now' the priest announced and made way for others to approach the body.

Reghu moved towards the body and kissed the forehead. Reghu's eyes and face were down in the dumps.

After the last rites the priest took a white towel and placed it on the face of Johnson and directed to take the body.

Two people took the body and lowered it inside the grave by using ropes.

Priest then took some wet soil and dropped it slowly into the grave. Few other people did the same.

Some workers covered the grave with soil and closed it.

After some prayers people went out of the cemetery with a gloomy face, But Reghu stayed staring at the grave.

#

Reghu took his Audi A8 and went to the police station near Seawoods.

Reghu reached the police station, he parked his car and went inside the station. He went to the Sub-inspector's room.

'May I?' Reghu asked politely.

'Yes come in' SI said.

'Sir, I am Reghu Jadhav, friend of Advocate Johnson Xavier' Reghu said.

'Ok sir, how can I help you?' SI said.

'Can I know about what happened to Johnson?' Reghu said.

'Constable' SI called out loudly.

'Yes sir' one of the constables came inside.

'Show him the details of the Advocate's death' SI said. Constable nodded.

'Thank you sir'.

Reghu and the constable went out of SI's office and went to his desk.

'Have a seat sir' the constable said politely.

'Thank you' Reghu said and sat on one of the old wooden chairs.

The police station is old and has around 9 policemen. The walls are ragged and they haven't been painted in a long while. The prison cell was free and dark. All were busy in their own work.

The constable brought a file outside. It contains FIR, Photos from the Crime spot, etc....

'Sir, this is the way we found him near the station' the constable said by handing over a photo to Reghu.

The body was inside a sack tied up with a rope. The sack was full of blood and it was dried up. The body might have been sacked two days back.

'This was the condition of the body' Constable said and gave another photo.

The body was having a lot of scratches and deep wounds. His clothes were all torn up. He was tortured brutally before being murdered.

'His private organ was.....' constable paused.

'What's all this? It's a brutal murder with vengeance' Reghu broke.

'Yes sir, it is. We have a suspect but.....'

'Who is it? Why is he not detained yet?' Reghu asked furiously.

'Sir, please calm down. He is the father of Sruthi' the constable said.

'Who is Sruthi?' Reghu asked.

'She was raped by five youngsters and committed suicide last month' constable said.

'How did that have a connection with this murder?'

'Advocate Johnson saved those five brutal criminals' constable said and closed the file.

Reghu looked down and took a deep breath.

'And also the father of the girl had made a death threat towards Advocate Johnson on the day in the court, we have witnesses for that' constable said.

'Then why is he still not arrested?' Reghu asked in disappointment.

'We cannot arrest him only with this evidence' the constable said.

'Hmm' Reghu said disappointedly and stood up to leave.

Reghu took his purse and gave two thousand rupees to the constable. And went back to SI's room.

'Sir, he should be arrested at any cost' Reghu said.

'Yes, but need some more evidence as the public was very furious about the judgement of the rape case' SI said.

'Hmm' Reghu agreed.

'Sir, Advocate Johnson's family?' SI asked.

'They all died long back and he is not married' Reghu said.

'Sir, you can take this' SI said and handed over a key.

Reghu took the key and gave a glance at it. A car key with a shiny BMW logo. Reghu closed his eyes slowly.

CHAPTER THREE

Seven years back.

Reghu and Johnson were sitting on the couch at Reghu's house and watching a movie "Transporter". Reghu's father was sitting in the same room with his laptop.

Janson Statham comes in black suit with black tie in the BMW 735i on the screen.

'Wow, that's a powerful entry' Johnson said in enthusiasm.

'Yeah, really stylish' Reghu said.

'I will buy this car and I will come here wearing a black suit' Johnson said.

\#

On the day of convocation from Symbiosis Law College, Reghu and Johnson were wearing black suits and black tie with a gown over it, sitting in the front row with their friends.

'Our academic topper Mr. Johnson Xavier' principal announced proudly.

Johnson stood up and went towards the stage and took the gold medal from Reghu's grandpa who was the Mumbai High court judge at the time.

Johnson's face was glowing with happiness and gratitude.

After convocation, Reghu took him to the parking lot and gave him a key. He looked at the black key and saw a shiny BMW logo on it.

'For the topper' Reghu said and held his friend's shoulder.

He pressed the unlock button of the key and looked around for the response.

A sweet indicative noise came twice from the parking lot and headlamps flicked twice. Luxurious cars always have a unique sweet sound apart from other cars.

Johnson went near to the new BMW 735i and opened the door and sat inside. His eyes were glittering and he became speechless.

Reghu opened his eyes slowly and took a deep breath sitting on the driver's seat in the black BMW.

Reghu took Johnson's car and went back to his house. He parked the BMW and sent his driver to get his Audi from the police station.

Reghu went inside his house, and directly to his room. He fell on the bed and slept away. The happenings of the whole day made him exhausted.

'Reghu, did you go to the police station yesterday?' grandpa asked while waking him up from the bed.

Reghu woke up and looked at grandpa.

'Yes pa, I saw the photographs of his body, it was full of scratches, and blood.....the killer tortured him so much before killing. They have a suspect who had threatened him last month' Reghu said.

'Then what is the status' grandpa asked.

'They don't have much evidence to arrest him and the suspect is from a sensitive case which Johnson appeared before. Police cannot move forward without solid evidence' Reghu said.

'We need to find the truth' Grandpa said.

'How?' Reghu said, confused.

'I have called one of my students, she is good at this. She will find the truth and help in getting justice for Johnson' Grandpa said.

'Who is she?' Reghu said.

#

Reghu came downstairs from his room in the morning. He heard someone talking in the visitor's room. He headed towards the room.

Grandpa was talking to someone politely.

'Beta, good morning' Grandpa said when he saw Reghu coming from bed.

'Good morning pa' Reghu said, he was still sleepy.

'Reghu this is Amaana, my student and this is Reghu my only grandson' Grandpa said introducing both of them.

Reghu looked at Amaana and shook her hand.

Amaana was a beautiful young successful aspiring lawyer, she was from Punjab.

Reghu's eyes glittered. Her beauty made him forget everything happening around him. He stared deep into her beauty.

Reghu stood still and his eyes were on her.

Amaana was wearing a white shirt and skinny blue jeans. Her hair was open and was floating in the gentle breeze from the entrance door. She was wearing an antique earring, it was sparkling in the fresh sunlight.

'Hi Reghu, I'm Amaana Kaur' she said.

Her voice is sweet like Gulab Jamun. Reghu didn't respond and waited to hear more of her sweet voice.

'Hi' she said again.

'Hello, nice to meet you' Reghu said.

'Amaana, Johnson is Reghu's best friend, his death was really a shock for him' Grandpa said.

'Johnson was equal to Reghu for us. He was also our son' Grandpa said, looking at Amaana in a sad tone.

'Yes sir, I understand' she said.

'Reghu, will you accompany her?' Grandpa asked, facing

Reghu, who was still staring at her.

'Of course pa' Reghu said turning from her face.

\#

Reghu was waiting inside BMW outside Amaana's flat near Thane.

She was living in a flat near Upvan Lake. The place was very calm and it did not have any issues of Mumbai city. Reghu parked his car under a huge banyan tree, the leaves falling down as the wind passed by.

Reghu's phone beeped twice.

'Jus a min' Amaana messaged.

Reghu replied with a smiling emoticon.

After a few minutes, Amaana comes out of the lift.

She was wearing a blue salwar kameez with broad golden embroidery work on the end of the top. She looks prettier in ethnic wear than in modern.

'Are we going on a date?' Reghu thought and smiled towards her through the window.

She saw Reghu inside the car, she smiled back at Reghu.

When she smiles her jasmine petals make her more gorgeous, they are so cute that no one can resist her.

She reached near the car, opened the door and got inside. A special fragrance spread inside the BMW. That fragrance made Reghu speechless. He just enjoyed the fragrance for a moment.

'Hey Reghu' Amaana said, snapping her finger at his face.

Reghu woke up from the heavenly feeling.

'Sorry, nothing. Let's go?' Reghu asked.

'First we can go to the police station and take the details and let me study about the case in detail' she said like a professional.

CHAPTER FOUR

'Hey what happened? Is something bothering you?' Reghu asked with concern looking at her.

Her eyes were sparkling in the sunlight, she was wearing the advocate's black coat and white saree inside.

Reghu and Amaana were sitting in an outdoor coffee shop under an umbrella. The day for first examination of Advocate Johnson murder case.

'Nothing, I have a feeling that he is not the killer' she said with confusion. Her voice was not firm.

'Sir, order please' the waiter asked.

'What would you like to have?' Reghu said.

'Cappuccino' she said.

'Make it two' he said.

Waiter went back. Reghu looked back at her.

'All evidence is against him, then why?' Reghu asked with confidence.

'Yeah that's true but.... I don't know. My mind is messed up now' Amaana said, puzzled.

'Hey relax, everything is fine. Don't worry. We are on the right path' he said.

Reghu extended his arms and held her hand.

Amaana gazed with a smile.

'Sir, your cappuccino' waiter kept two cappuccino on the table gently.

The cappuccinos had a heart shape on its top with white

cream. Reghu moved one to her.

Reghu took the other cup and had a teeny sip.

Amaana started to laugh looking at his face, and pointed to his face.

Reghu suddenly kept his cup on the table and tried to take his towel. The towel took a minute to come out from his jeans pocket.

Amaana leaned forward and wiped his new moustache with her fingers. Reghu went speechless. Her fingers tickled his lips. It was like snow falling on his lips and abdomen. Both of them giggled.

After finishing their lovely cappuccinos. They started their journey to the court.

'You want to drive?' Reghu asked. She refused softly.

'Still it bothers you?' Reghu asked.

'No... I'm fine' she said and continued.

'Hey, wait, what will you give me if we win this case?' Amaana asked in a naughty tone.

'It's a surprise, I won't tell you right now' Reghu said while driving.

'Hey, tell yaar...' she said and pinched Reghu softly on his muscular biceps.

'Oooww, it hurts' Reghu reacted and smiled at her naughtiness.

They reached Bombay session's court. As usual media is ready to attack, they stood there like zombies to bite with unnecessary questions.

Amaana took a file from the dashboard and went straight into BAR. Amaana didn't respond to any questions from the media. Reghu parked his BMW and went inside the court, taking a comfortable seat. Some other cases were going on.

\#

A police van arrived at the entrance of the court. A white

Gypsy with rotating blue light.

Two policemen came out with a man from the back. He looked terrible, he looked like he didn't sleep for a decade. Tired eyes, guilty face and shabby dress, he was totally done. Police took him inside the court.

A white Maruti 800 came inside the court and went directly to the parking area. A middle aged man came out of the car. He has white hair and old spectacles, carries his gown on his shoulder and some files in his left hand.

Advocate Nandha Gopal, an activist who works for the poor who doesn't have money to spend on expensive advocates. He has been appointed as the defender for the suspect by the BAR council of Mumbai.

'Sir, will Johnson get justice?' one reporter asked with her mic on Nandha Gopal.

'Yes, truth should win.' Advocate Nandha Gopal said.

'Sir, will Dhinesh get the death sentence?' another reporter asked.

'No comments' Advocate Nandha Gopal cut the questions and left the entrance.

\#

Mumbai sessions court.

Court was filled with public, Advocates were sitting in front. Advocate Nandha Gopal entered the court and took his seat opposite to Amaana.

Amaana gazed at Reghu. Reghu gestured her "all the best" with his right thumb up. Amaana smiled at his gesture.

Judge entered the court after a recess. He took his seat at the podium and opened laptop on his table.

'Session case numbers one thousand two hundred seven bar three thousand one' clerk called out.

'May I proceed, my lord?' Amaana asked the Judge.

'Please' Judge permitted.

Amaana walked slowly towards the suspect box, where Dhinesh was standing. He was broke, half dead.

'Mr. Dhinesh, How do you know Johnson Xavier?' she asked looking at his dead eyes.

'Sir, Advocate Johnson was the criminal lawyer in my daughter's case' Dhinesh replied with a low voice. He did not have the energy to raise his voice.

'What was the judgement of that case?' Amaana asked.

'Johnson sir saved those brutal criminals, who raped my daughter and threw her as garbage' Dhinesh said and started sobbing.

'My lord, please give permission for examining Witness number one' Amaana courteously bowed.

'Permission granted' Judge said.

'Witness number one Advocate Shanaya' clerk called loudly.

Advocate Shanaya walked slowly to the witness box and bowed to the judge.

'Miss. Shanaya, How long have you been working with Advocate Johnson as his assistant?' Amaana asked.

'Thirteen months' Shanaya said.

'Can you please say in detail what happened in the court on that day of final judgement of Mumbai rape case' advocate asked.

'After the judgement all moved out of the court, me and Johnson sir was moving out of the court, suddenly this man blocked us and threatened him saying that he will kill him' Shanaya said very authentically.

'Objection my lord' Advocate Nandha Gopal said and continued.

Amaana looked at Advocate Nandha Gopal.

the Judge said, ``Objection sustained'

'My lord, here I submit the CCTV footage in the court as

the evidence of this statement. That's all my lord' Amaana completed her statement and went back to her seat.

Clerk gave CCTV footage to the Judge. Judge played it on his laptop. He waited until the video was completed.

'This footage tells that there was a threat conversation between Dhinesh and Advocate Johnson' Judge said and continued.

'Defence you may proceed' Judge commanded.

'My lord, if Dhinesh was having revenge he would have killed those five teenagers first, why advocate Johnson alone? The police cooked up this and tried to close the case on a poor person like Dhinesh and hide the real killer' Advocate said.

'Objection my lord' Amaana said and stood up.

She was looking so beautiful in that black gown. Her voice was firm and bold.

'My lord, the defender is taking advantage of emotions here. The death threat alone will not prove this case, but I have more evidence to prove that Mr. Dhinesh accomplished his threat.' Amaana said and walked towards her table and took two papers. And continued.

'My lord, this is the location track of Advocate Johnson's mobile phone when it was switched on last and this is the location track of Mr. Dhinesh at the exact same time. The information is based on the cyber security force.' Amaana said and handed over the two papers to the judge through the clerk and continued.

'Both advocate and Dhinesh were under the same tower location. This can be a proof for their meeting at Johnson's last moments.' Amaana said and went back to her chair.

Judge took the wooden hammer and gently hit it on the table and looked towards the public.

'The judgement of this case is moved to December thirty

first 2017' Judge said.

Police took the suspect out of the box.

Reghu came out of the courtroom and joined Amaana who was waiting for him outside.

'Wow...what a performance man' Reghu said smiling and gave hands to her.

'That's me' Amaana said and raised her left eyebrow twice.

'So cute, show that again' Reghu asked.

'No, I won't' she said.

'I will make you' Reghu said and tickled on her navel through the gap of her white saree.

'Stop it Reghu, people are watching' Amaana said and held Reghu's hand and giggled.

CHAPTER FIVE

31 December 2017.

'Mr. Dhinesh, father of Mumbai rape case victim got Death sentence for Advocate Johnson murder case' one reporter said looking to the camera.

Amaana and Reghu came out of the court and the media blocked them.

Reporters were asking lots of questions to Amaana. Reghu pushes them away and cleared a way for her towards the car. They got inside the BMW and drove out of the court premise.

'Reghu, so I completed my task, don't forget the surprise' Amaana said.

'Hey, are you joining our new year party?' Reghu asked.

'Are you going to finish the treat with that, then I will kill you.'

'You don't trust me?' he asked.

'No.... I'm just kidding' she giggled.

They rode back to Reghu's house. Grandpa was waiting for them outside the house.

'Aaja beta, Congrats, you performed well' Grandpa said and hugged Amaana.

After hugging Amaana gazed at Reghu with a smile.

'Thank you, sir'

'Stop calling me sir' Grandpa said

'Ok pa' she replied and giggled.

'Congrats you did well beti' Dhamodhar said with pride.
'Thanks dad' she said.
'Let's have lunch?' Dhamodhar asked.
'Yeah, I'm starving' Reghu said and went inside the house.
A fantastic lunch was already prepared for them. The large dining table was full of a variety of dishes from around the world. Amaana got surprised and became speechless by seeing the table. Reghu held her on shoulders from behind and pushed her gently towards a seat next to his, pulled a wooden classy chair for her and made her comfortable.
Reghu took the seat next to her and blinked his eyes at her with a smile. They had lunch together.
'Reghu can you drop me at my flat' Amaana requested. Reghu nodded when he was finishing his desert.
They took their BMW and went to her flat.
'Reghu, come let's have tea' Amaana asked after getting out of the car outside her flat.
'Okay, let me see your space' Reghu agreed and came out of the car.
Reghu and Amaana walked together and stepped inside the elevator. They both were in deep silence inside the elevator.
They got out of it and Reghu followed her towards her flat.
'Nice flat, really cute like you' Reghu said after exploring the rooms.
The rooms had some paintings and decorations. She had a small library which was full of law books. Reghu turned away when he saw those heavy dark hard covers.
'I'm feeling lazy to make a Tea, let's have some wine either' Amaana asked for permission, Reghu nodded.
Amaana went to the shelf where crystal glasses were kept. The glasses were so beautiful and were glittering with the passing sunlight of the sunset. She took two wine glasses

and a bottle of Sula Rasa and sat next to Reghu on the couch.

'Here is your Drink' Amaana said and gave a half glass of wine to Reghu.

'Skol' both brought their glasses near and made a gentle touch.

Reghu raised the glass for a toast.

'To my best friend Johnson and to my dear Amaana who gave justice to his soul' Reghu said and kept the glass on the table.

Reghu got a little emotional. He covered his face in order to hide his tears for his best friend.

Amaana kept her glass aside and held Reghu to her shoulder.

'Hey Reghu, what's this?' Amaana asked with concern.

'He was the only friend I had and he left me alone in this world' Reghu said, pressing his face to Amaana's shoulder.

'Alone...who said? You have a great family and I. You didn't even think of me' Amaana said and held his face in her soft hands and looked at his wet eyes.

'Thank you' Reghu said and looked back at Amaana's eyes.

They moved closer. Their eyes stayed connected. Their hearts started to beat so fast. Their lips touched each other. They started to smell the intense romantic fragrance of each other.

Reghu moved Amaana's hair from her face with his left hands. She held him closer to her bosom with her hands.

Their lips refused to move apart. They connected for long time.

Reghu leaned towards her and made her lay on the couch. His hands wrapped her.

Reghu moved his lips to give a soft bite on her right ear.

'I love you' Reghu whispered in her ears. Amaana got

tickled when his breath brushed her and she tilted her neck to the shoulder with a silly smile.

Amaana giggled and held him tighter to her body. She moved her hands through his hair and pulled his lips back to her and they kissed for several minutes.

#

They both were on the couch, Amaana was lying on his chest sleeping. Reghu was brushing her hair and gazing at her cuteness.

Suddenly Reghu looked at his watch. He got a little worried. He held Amaana's shoulders and raised her. She got a little uncomfortable.

'What happened?' she asked when she noticed his hurry.

'I need to go, you go fresh up and I will pick you up for the party' Reghu said while searching for his car keys.

Reghu left Amaana's flat in a hurry.

She got up from the couch and went to the washroom. She looked in the mirror and started laughing and dancing. She was dancing out of mind. She took off her clothes, and went under the shower. Water flowed through her whole body.

After the luxurious bath, she opened her wooden wardrobe. It was full of expensive costumes. She took a long look on the entire suit and her eyes locked at a glittering solid black bodycon dress. She turned towards the mirror and held the black bodycon in front of her and gave a silly smile.

'Reghu, I love you too' Amaana said, looking in the mirror and giggled.

Her phone cried with a message. She eagerly took the phone. A message from Reghu on the notification.

'R u ready dear, I'm on my way.'

Reghu reached the gate of her flat. Reghu dialled her number. Waited desperately for her to pick up.

She didn't answer. Reghu called again and again. No response. "The person you are calling is not answering, please call after some time" the lady kept informing on each call.

Reghu came out of the car with a petrified face. He walked briskly to her flat. He rang the bell twice, no response.

Reghu gently touched the door but the door was open. The room was dark, no lights. His heart started to beat fast. His eyes moved to all corners in the dark.

Reghu found a switch board by the moonlight coming through the long glass window. He went near the switch board slowly and switched on all the switches it have.

'Taadaa' Amaana said standing at the door of her bedroom with the glittering black bodycon dress and a Hermes Birkin's noir handbag on her left hand.

Amaana looks so hot in bodycon, her dress ends at her thighs. Reghu got really surprised and his eyes went down to her beautifully waxed shiny legs.

'Are you trying to make us late for the party?' Reghu said as he was enjoying her beauty.

'Stop staring at me, Reghu' Amaana said.

'You are so hot, I can't resist' Reghu said and walked ploddingly near to her with a naughty face.

'So I'm irresistible, huh?' She said with a silly smile on her face.

Reghu put his hands behind her and pulled her towards him. Her bosom hit his chest. Reghu and Amaana touched their foreheads together and looked eyes to eyes.

'Party....' Amaana whispered.

'Yeah, yeah' Reghu said and slowly took his hands off of her. They got inside the car and went to Prive night club near Colaba beach. The party had already begun; Reghu was in a black hoodie and blue jeans.

They entered the club, fully packed, all in a great mood, dancing with the DJ. Reghu and Amaana went near the bartender.

'Mojito and you' Reghu ordered looking at Amaana.

'Pina colada' Amaana said.

'Oh that's cool.'

The bartender took a glass bottle from behind and started preparing the drink. He took the bottle and threw it several times and poured it into a long blue glass. He took a classy wine glass and poured the cocktail slowly into it and placed a red cherry on the glass.

'Ma'am, your Pina colada' the bartender said after serving the drink.

He started to make Mojito by throwing another bottle and poured to another glass and placed a lemon slice on it.

'Sir, your Mojito', the bartender said.

Reghu and Amaana took their glasses and cheered. Both of them took one sip and moved towards a table in the corner.

'Hey Reghu, come join us' a guy on the dance floor cried out loudly.

'Yeah, come let's dance' Reghu asked Amaana. They went to the dance floor hand in hand. Music changed one after another, they danced together.

'Reghu, it's 11:40 let's head out' Amaana said.

'It's going to be New Year in a few minutes' Reghu said.

'I want to be out in a peaceful place with you on 12' Amaana said looking in his eyes.

They left the club and walked to the beach. They walked through the soft sand. Amaana was holding her heels in her left hand.

'Clear sky with a lot of stars, all are trying to hit on this hot girl' Reghu said.

Amaana pinch Reghu's left biceps and put her hands

through his left hand and laid her head on his shoulder and continued walking.

A cracker came into the sky. It lit up their eyes

'It's new year' Amaana said and jumped high and looked at Reghu.

Reghu was on his knees.

'Will you be my companion for celebrating hundreds of new years like this' Reghu proposed by holding an opened ring box.

An elegant glittering diamond ring. The reflection of the fireworks in the sky makes the ring more beautiful and precious.

Amaana got really surprised. Her face glowed. Her eyes were wide open.

'Really?' Amaana asked and she came down on her knees with Reghu.

Her face was glittering with intense happiness. She showed her left hand to Reghu. Reghu took the ring and put on her beautiful ring finger. Amaana leaned towards Reghu and kissed him on the lips.

Under the sky, witnessing millions of stars and lights from fireworks, they kissed for a long time.

CHAPTER SIX

'Good morning' Reghu said to grandpa and his dad, they were sitting in the living room.

'Good morning beta' Grand pa said.

'Good morning son, when you are returning to New York' Dhamodhar asked.

'Yeah, I was about to tell you, but before that I wanted to discuss another important matter' he said little seriously.

Grandpa took his eyes from the news paper and looked at Reghu curiously through his reading glasses.

'I'm in love with Amaana, I would like to marry her' Reghu said in a low voice.

'Wow that is great news. Does she know about it? grandpa asked surprisingly.

'Yeah she knows and yesterday I proposed her too' Reghu said enthusiastically.

'Oh, everything is going so fast' Dhamodhar said.

'Son, let's move forward with this, she is a good kid. You both have good chemistry' grandpa added for convincing Dhamodhar.

'Okay, I don't have any obligation let's move ahead with it' Dhamodhar agreed.

Reghu came near Dhamodhar and grandpa, gave a hug and went upstairs to his room, in a thrill.

'I told you, how was my idea, it worked' grandpa said.

'You are genius in these matters, you are a better broker

than a Judge' Dhamodhar said to grandpa with a silly smile. Grandpa raised his right hand to mock a hit on his son for teasing him with a smile.

Reghu entered his room and fell on his bed backward. His face was glowing like a full moon. Reghu leaned towards a fluffy pillow and hugged it, pretending her on his mind.

Reghu took his phone and messaged Amaana.

'Today eveng five, Starbucks, I want to see you' Reghu messaged.

#

Reghu was waiting in the Starbucks coffee shop. A European styled, classy Coffee shop. People from different places were having their delightful beverages. Some were having chats with their colleagues with coffee, some others were using laptops and working, some were reading books and some were waiting for someone else like Reghu. A perfect peaceful place to spend the evening and get relaxed. Amaana comes in her small cute blue Brio and parked in front of the Cafe. She was wearing a plain lavender salwar kameez with cowl neck. She always does the simple eyeliner which manifests her glittering eyes more vividly.

Amaana entered the cafe and looked for Reghu. He was sitting in the right corner. Amaana saw him and walked towards him with a cute smile on her face.

'Sorry, am I late?' Amaana asked.

'No, I was just reading this book' Reghu said and showed her a novel named "He is mine".

'Oh, it's a great time stealer. I like this book' she said looking at the cover.

'I had a conversation with my dad and grandpa yesterday' Reghu said.

'About what?' she asked.

'About us, yaar.'

'Oh, sorry, then what did they say?' she asked curiously.

Reghu stayed with a sad face. She noticed his expression and didn't feel comfortable. They looked at each other for a moment.

'What happened?' Amaana asked without patience.

Reghu's face started to change slowly from sad to smiling.

'They are so excited about us' Reghu said, breaking the suspense.

Amaana's face was glowing with happiness. Reghu held her soft hands gently.

'I will be with you forever' Reghu promised.

'Me too, I need a hug' Amaana said and extended both hands towards Reghu.

Reghu came closer to her and hugged with immense happiness.

'But, I'm leaving you' Reghu said in a bold voice in her ears.

'What?' she said and pushed him off of her and looked in his eyes.

'I'm leaving for New York, my business, you forgot' Reghu asked.

Amaana breathed out as he said that.

'Oh that, you always keep everything a suspense nowadays, I don't really like it' she said.

'When you are leaving for Punjab, will your mom and dad be ok with our relationship?' Reghu asked anxiously.

'My mom and dad are not orthodox, they always support my dreams' she said.

'So we are getting married, Wow I can't believe this! All of this happened so fast' Reghu said excitedly.

#

'I'm leaving tomorrow, I will miss you' Reghu said with a sad face.

Reghu and Amaana were having dinner at her flat. The

room was in grave silence. They barely spoke. They were having butter naan and paneer masala.

'I will also miss you' Amaana said.

'When are you leaving for Punjab?' he asked while making conversation.

'Day after tomorrow' she said.

All questions and answers were so low and they gave answers and kept themselves silent.

'Everything will be alright, I can't wait to have you' Reghu said.

'Wait, Mr. Covetous' Amaana said and put a silly smile on her face intentionally.

Reghu gave her back a smile and took another piece of Butter naan.

She was in a royal blue saree. She was looking like an actress who came to receive her Best actress award on TV.

After completing dinner Amaana took Butter scotch Ice cream from the refrigerator. Reghu was standing on the balcony looking at the silent lake. Amaana came to the balcony with the Ice cream in one bowl with two spoons.

'Ice cream for cooling you down' she said.

Cool breeze touched her soft hair. Her hair was moving with the breeze. Reghu looked at her hair which was gliding in the evening breeze.

'Hello' she called with a snap. He suddenly got distracted from the rhythmic movement of her hair to her eyes.

Reghu came closer to her. He caressed his finger on her left antique ear ring and his finger moved to cheek. She closed her eyes and felt his fingers.

She opened her eyes and saw Reghu was eating butter scotch ice cream horribly.

'You idiot, I will show you' she said and gave a gentle pinch on his hand.

She gave a cute sad face and turned to the other side of the balcony.

Reghu smiled at her and hugged her from behind. Reghu gave a sweet bite on her neck. She got tickled and gently moved her head. She turned around to face him. Both kissed passionately in that cool breeze and moon light.

Reghu and Amaana in a BMW on the way to Mumbai international airport. Both of them were in silence. They reached the airport.

Reghu was wearing a black T-shirt and holding a Black jacket on his left hand and a small trolley bag on his right. Amaana accompanied Reghu to the entrance.

'I will miss you, One month will be horrible for me' Reghu said with a sad face, holding her hand.

'Me too, come fast I'm waiting for you' Amaana said.

'Final call for flight number G825 to New York' announcement came from a speaker.

They looked with disappointment to the direction of the source of sound.

'Bye' Reghu said and leaned forward to Amaana and gave her a kiss on the lips.

'Bye' Amaana said with pain.

Reghu took his trolley and walked away from Amaana to gate 121. Amaana waved her hands and waited for Reghu to get away from her sight.

CHAPTER SEVEN

New York City

Reghu was wearing a black jacket and was holding his trolley in his left hand. It was cold in New York. He came out through the arrival gate in JFK New York Airport.

One white blonde girl was waiting at the exit. She was wearing a grey women's suit. She had a cream shawl on her neck. Smooth silky open hair.

She waved at Reghu. Reghu noticed her and walked towards her.

'Hey, sweetheart, miss you a lot' Reghu said and hugged her.

'I too, how was India?' She asked.

'As usual, dust and traffic' Reghu said.

'Ok let's leave, we have a meeting with a new client. You have to be there' she said professionally.

Both walked to the parking, and got inside a Royal blue Mini cooper convertible car. She drove the car out of the parking lot.

'I'm back in my heaven' Reghu said relaxed.

'You can freshen up and I will come and pick you up after an hour. Is that okay?' She asked.

'No way, I will come in my Huracan' Reghu disagreed.

'Oh, so don't ask for my ride at night' She said.

'Pat, you look so adorable when angry, my cutie' Reghu said and pinched on her soft cheeks.

'You are a bad boy' Pat said.

Pat stopped the car in front of a white painted house with black roof. Reghu got out of the Cooper and walked to the driver side and knocked on the glass.

Pat opened the glass. Reghu laid his hands on the door and leaned inside the car.

'Hey look at my eyes' Reghu said.

Pat looked into his eyes.

'Love you' he said and moved forward to her lips and they kissed.

\#

Reghu got inside the meeting hall with Pat. He was in a black suit and red tie. Pat was carrying a suitcase. All others stood up as he got inside the room. Reghu went to his special seat at the centre.

'All, please be seated' Reghu said with authority.

Pat handed over the suitcase to him. Reghu opened it and took some documents out.

'Good morning, we have gone through all the documents and understood that this is a sinking ship and you guys cannot sail anymore' he said and stood up.

All the faces went doubtful.

'But I'm interested in your firm, still not good with the figure' Reghu said disappointed.

'Sir, it's negotiable' one among them said quickly.

'It has to, because I will not get anything from it, an old analytics company' Reghu said.

'Sir, your Deal?' a Japanese man said.

'Twenty million' he said.

'Sir, that's low' the Japanese man said.

'Look Mr.???' Reghu said, looking at the Japanese man.

'Chiug Ling' the Japanese man said.

'Yeah, Mr. Chiug Lin, I'm buying this for my company's

business strategy, I can recruit some freshers and do this job but if I get people who know about it, it will be much better so, that's it' Reghu said in a bold voice.

'Sir can we have a private conversation?' Chiug Lin asked Reghu.

His English accent was very different, but very cute to hear. Reghu looked at Pat. She showed them the way to a mini meeting room and closed the door from outside.

'Reghu, do we require a company for our business?' Pat asked in confusion.

'Pat, we don't need external help to know our market, this is different' Reghu said.

'Yeah, you are only required for market study' she said.

Reghu closed one eye with a silly smile.

'Then why twenty million?' Pat asked.

'I'm going to start a new business' Reghu said.

Pat was surprised.

'Analytics, we have companies for analysing the market, weather, etc. We are going to analyse the people through their personal data and social media.' Reghu said.

'For what' Pat said.

'For developing special strategies for elections, amendments and other government matters' Reghu said.

'Wow, you are next level' Pat said with an amused face.

'I will discuss with you later in detail' Reghu said.

'They are coming' Pat said looking towards the mini meeting hall.

Chiug Lin and others came out of the Mini hall and took their seats. Reghu sat still on his chair and was using his phone without giving any attention to the People.

'Sir, we are ready for the deal' Chiug Lin said in dissatisfaction.

'That's good' Reghu said and extended his hand towards

Chiug Lin.
They both shook their hands.
'Pat, please accompany them for the formalities' Reghu requested.
She showed them the way out. The Japanese people got out of the meeting room. Pat came back to Reghu.
'So tonight, party' Pat asked.
'As you wish majesty' Reghu said and moved closer to Pat.
Reghu moved his hand to her butt and pressed gently and pushed her closer. Their lips came closer and Reghu's mobile ringed.
Reghu stopped and moved back looking at the phone. Amaana calling...
#
'Hey sweetheart' Reghu picked up the call...
'How was the flight?' Amaana asked.
'Flight was safe but boring, I really missed you' Reghu said walking inside his cabin.
'Then, did you have lunch?' Amaana asked with concern.
'No, I was in a meeting with a client' Reghu said.
'It's getting late, I had my dinner' Amaana said.
'You ate without me, right' Reghu said with a silly angry tone.
'Sorry, come I will give you lunch' Amaana said.
'Don't talk to me' Reghu is still keeping a sad tone.
'Sorry, sorry, sorry' Amaana apologized.
'Just kidding' Reghu said.
'Still, sorry' she said.
'Yeah ok, so you are going to sleep' he said.
'Yeah, tired' she said.
'So okay Good night' he said.
'Don't go, I want a kiss' she said.
'Only one?' he asked.

'Give me my kisses' she said in a romantic tone.

Reghu made kiss sounds on the mic with a silly smile on his face.

'I got everything' she said.

'So you are not giving me' Reghu asked and waited for her kisses.

'Got it, okay good night dear' Reghu said.

'Good night, I want you' Amaana said.

'Miss you.'

'Miss you too' she replied.

Reghu hung up the call and opened the gallery inside his mobile and looked at their selfie.

Pat came inside Reghu's cabin with a file.

'Everything's fine, we are ready to launch the new business' Pat said enthusiastically.

Reghu smiled at her and signed on the papers.

'So let's go for lunch' Reghu said.

'Yeah, I'm starving' Pat said.

They walked together towards the canteen. The whole Japanese group was there having their lunch. The dining table was well decorated and waiters were coming with different types of foods and dishes. Reghu and Pat took their seats and started their lunch.

'Don't forget the party, tonight' she whispered in his ears.

'Let's rock it babe, where do you want to go?' Reghu asked.

'10ak' Pat said looking to Reghu's eyes.

'Oh so you are in a great mood' he said and gave a naughty look at her.

#

Reghu's phone beeped,

'Hey' message from Amaana.

'Why so early, it will be around 4 AM over there, right?' Reghu replied.

'My train is early' phone beeped.
'So all the best and safe journey' Reghu messaged back.
Amaana thanked. Mobile beeped two more times.
'Miss you'.
'Love you, come back soon'
'Love you dear' Reghu texted back.
Reghu kept his phone on the table and concentrated on his black tie.
Phone beeped again. Reghu took the phone.
'Hey I'm ready, come pick me up boss' message from Pat.
'Yeah, on my way babe' Reghu texted back.
Reghu was wearing a black suit and a black tie. He looked at the mirror for setting his hair. He took his favourite perfume Jovan Musk from the small drawer near to the clear mirror.
Reghu took his Huracan and drove towards Pat's place. On the way to her home he stopped at a flower shop and picked up a bouquet of Red roses. He reached her house and parked his car and got out with fresh Red roses.
Reghu walked towards her door, and rang the bell. A melodious sound came from inside. Pat came near the door. Reghu's mobile beeped.
'Finally I'm on my train' Amaana texted. Reghu saw the message, but couldn't reply for it.
Pat opened the door.
'Wow, Red roses' Pat said.
'This for my queen' Reghu said and gave her the bouquet.
They hugged. Reghu's mobile beeped again.
'Are you busy, are you awake?' Amaana texted.
Reghu didn't reply. He was taken inside by Pat holding his left hand. Pat made him sit on the couch.
'Five minutes' Pat said and went inside her dressing room.
Reghu took his phone and messaged Amaana.

'No yaar, I'm fine, you are comfortable right?' Reghu texted.

'Yeah I'm going to have a small nap everyone on the train is asleep' Amaana texted.

'Good night, love you' Reghu messaged.

'Love you' Amaana replied with a hugging smiley.

'Hey busy boy' Pat said.

Reghu locked his phone and looked towards her.

'Wow, you look hot' Reghu exclaimed.

Pat was wearing a Royal red lengthy bodycon with thigh split. Her legs are shining in the dim light inside her living room.

'Shut your mouth you idiot. Let's go' Pat said and closed Reghu's mouth gently with her long pointing finger.

Reghu stood up and caught her hands and pulled her to him.

'Are you from Wonderland, princess?' Reghu asked by touching her lips with his fingers?

Her lips were glittering, Reghu's hand wrapped her and pulled her more closely and they stood looking into each other's eyes and Reghu moved forward. Pat moved her lips towards Reghu's. Their lips reached a heartbeat away.

Reghu's phone beeped. Reghu suddenly moved back.

'Good night, sweet dreams' Amaana's message.

Reghu kept mobile inside his pocket and looked back. Pat was near the door.

'Hey what are you waiting for lets go' Pat said.

#

Reghu and pat were sleeping at her house. They were cuddled under a white blanket. The bedroom was so pretty that everyone will get romantic.

The sunlight came through the wall window. A digital clock shows nine twenty three in red digits. Suddenly Reghu's phone started ringing. Reghu slowly moved his hand for the mobile. Pat woke up as he moved to her, but she went back to sleep again.

Reghu took his phone and looked, it was a video call from Amaana.

'Oh sh..' Reghu said without completing.

He moved slowly and gently from the bed by concentrating on Pat, whether she is waking or not. He moved out of the bed and went to the balcony.

Reghu took the video call.

'Hi Good morning, did I disturb you?' Amaana asked.

She tied her hair in a ponytail and had a small black round bindi on her forehead.

'Hey no, I was awake' Reghu said.

'I told my parents about us' she said.

'Oh, then what?' He said.

'They are very happy about us' she said with joy.

'Wow, great, so we are getting married' Reghu said with excitement.

'Yeah, yeah' she replied in joy.

'So what is your plan?' Reghu said.

'Let's move on, tell papa to arrange for Haldi' she said.

'I will come back soon, and let's get married, I can't wait any more to conquer you' Reghu said in a kingly tone.

'Me too, Love you, love you' she said and gave a kiss.

'Miss you' Reghu said and gave a kiss back to her.

Reghu cut the phone and went back inside. Pat was still in the bed. Reghu jumped to the bed and Pat woke up. Reghu went near her and kissed on her forehead.

'What happened?' Pat panicked.

'Nothing, I'm leaving for India next week' Reghu said.

'Why so fast?' she asked.

'Grandpa wants me there' Reghu said.

'Hmm, I will arrange the tickets for you' Pat said and got

up from the bed with the blanket wrapped around her. She walked to her dressing room. Reghu took his phone and dialled his grandpa.

'Ha beta, How are you?' Grandpa said through the phone.

'Pa, Amaana's family is also happy about our relationship' Reghu said.

'Oh, that is good news' Grandpa said.

'Dad is there?' he asked.

'Yeah, I'm hearing. Congratulations my boy' Dhamodhar said.

'Dad, I'm coming home next week. We need to arrange a Haldi and make this official' Reghu said.

'My boy all will be ready here.' Dhamodhar said.

'Okay, Love you guys' Reghu said and hung up.

CHAPTER EIGHT

Mumbai

Reghu took his mobile and called Amaana. Her phone was out of coverage. Reghu tried again and again. She was still out of coverage.

'Reghu, where is Dhamodhar?' grandpa asked in search of his son.

'Dad may be out for something, for some arrangements of tomorrow's function' Reghu said and looked back to his mobile.

'Any problem beta?' grandpa asked.

'No pa, Amaana and her family are on the way to Mumbai, so I'm trying to reach her' Reghu said.

'Vehicles for them?' grandpa asked.

'All set pa, I have already called and reminded our event coordinator, he will look after that' Reghu said.

Reghu again dialled her. She was still out of coverage.

Reghu went to the hotel to catch up on the progress in decoration. He saw the event coordinator Sony directing some boys to fix curtains. Reghu moved towards him.

'Hey Sony' Reghu called.

'Ha ji' Sony replied.

'All set?' Reghu said and looked at his watch.

'Yes sir, we will finish the job tonight itself' Sony said.

Sony turned to the boys and said to transfer the curtains.

Reghu looked again in his watch and called Sony.

'Did my dad come here?' Reghu asked.

'No, sir' Sony said.

Reghu took his mobile and called Dhamodhar. The mobile was out of coverage.

'All are out of the coverage area' Reghu said frustrated and cut the phone.

Reghu left the hotel and went to the parking lot. His phone rang while getting inside the BMW. It was Amaana.

'Hey, finally I got you' Reghu picked up and said.

'What happened?' Amaana asked.

'Nothing, where are you now?' Reghu asked.

'I reached my flat' Amaana said.

'I have arranged a car for you' Reghu said.

'Oh, sorry I didn't know that, we booked two cabs' Amaana said.

'Okay, how was the trip, is everyone Okay' he asked.

'Yeah fine, all are freshening up' she said.

'Do I need to be there to welcome them?' Reghu asked.

'No, all are tired, will go to bed soon, we can meet tomorrow and that would be better' Amaana said.

'Yeah, that's true, let them have some rest' he agreed.

'So let me fresh up and get some sleep' she said

'Ok babe, don't be late tomorrow ok, I want to see you as soon as possible' Reghu said.

'Ok dear, miss you, bye, and good night' Amaana said.

'Ok bye, good night' Reghu said and hung up.

Reghu drove the car to the Manyavar shop at Thane to collect his clothes for tomorrow which he had given for altering after the long shopping.

Reghu parked in front of the store and went inside. He gave the token and the salesman went inside to get the package.

After a few minutes, the salesman came and handed over a package. Reghu opened it and went on to try it inside the trial room.

Reghu came out with a splendid green Indo-western with mandarin collar. The dress was a perfect fit for him. Reghu went to the mirror and looked at himself. He took his mobile and took a selfie and sent it to Amaana.

Reghu's phone beeped.

'My dulha is hot and sexy' Amaana texted after viewing his photo.

Reghu saw the message and laughed loudly. Suddenly he looked around the shop and became silent. Reghu changed, packed it and went back home.

Reghu reached home and searched for Dad. Still he is not at home. He called again on his number. Still out of coverage.

'Shit, where is he?' Reghu asked in frustration and put his phone inside his pocket.

Reghu's phone started ringing. He took the phone from his pocket. It was an unknown number. He picked up the call.

'Hello' Reghu said.

'Hello, is this Reghu Jadhav?' the other person on the phone asked.

'Yes Reghu Jadhav here' he said.

'Reghu, I'm calling from Thane Nagar police station' the policeman said.

#

Reghu went to the Thane Nagar police station with grandpa. Reghu parked the car and helped grandpa get out of the car by opening the door. Reghu and grandpa walked slowly inside the police station.

They went directly to the Sub Inspector's room. When they entered inside, SI stood up and came near grandpa and gave a salute.

'Come sir, have a seat' SI said and moved one chair for grandpa and went back to his place.

'What happened sir, why did you call us?' Reghu asked.

'Both of you please be calm, I have terrible news for you' SI said and put his cap on the table. His face was gloomy and sad.

'Sir, please tell the matter' Reghu said.

'We got a body from Yeoor river, today evening and.......it's Mr. Dhamodhar's' SI said with a scorn on his face.

'What are you saying?' Grandpa said and stood up suddenly.

Reghu got stuck and got speechless. His eyes became red and face got pale.

'Reghu, get up beta' grandpa said and looked at Reghu. He didn't respond.

Grandpa asked SI's help and raised Reghu from the seat. Reghu went totally numb. With help of a police man they reached back home. Reghu was motionless.

Grandpa sat next to Reghu and hugged him. His eyes were filled with tears. Reghu's mobile started to ring. Grandpa took it. It was Amaana.

'Reghu, what happened?' Amaana asked.

'Beta, it's me' Grandpa said in a plain voice.

'Grandpa, what happened?' Amaana asked.

'Your dad went without blessing you children' Grandpa said and started to cry on the phone.

Amaana cut the call. Grandpa laid his head on Reghu's shoulder weeping.

The driver came inside.

'Sir?' Driver asked.

'Do the arrangements' grandpa said.

The driver turned back and went outside with a gloomy face. Reghu didn't move an inch. They remained there for several minutes.

Amaana came to Reghu's house, and found Reghu and

grandpa on the couch motionless. When grandpa saw Amaana, he raised his head from Reghu's shoulder.

'Beta' grandpa called.

Amaana went near them and sat down with them.

'Beta, can you take Reghu upstairs, he is not speaking' grandpa said.

'Okay pa' Amaana said and took Reghu by holding his shoulder. They went upstairs slowly.

Some people heard about the death and reached the house to express their condolences. An ambulance approached the gate. Grandpa went to the door and looked at the ambulance.

Ambulance came inside the gate and moved slowly to the porch. One man came outside from the driver's seat and went to the back of the ambulance. He opened the two doors wide out and he pulled one stretcher out. Dhamodhar's body was covered with white cloth.

Grandpa turned his face away. Another person came out of the ambulance holding the other end. They went inside the house with the cold still body. They kept the body in the guest room inside the freezer.

The whole guest room was covered with white curtains. The freezer was decorated with white Gladiolus flowers.

Amaana came out of the room with Reghu and came down, made him sit next to the body of his father. Reghu looked slowly at Dad's cold face. Tears came out from Reghu's eyes.

The head was tied with a white cloth, after Autopsy. Reghu sat there near his dad's body without noticing the people that came to give their condolences.

CHAPTER NINE

Reghu, Amaana, grandpa and few people were standing near the Dhamodhar's body. The body was on an iron stretcher at an electric crematorium near Ashok Nagar.

A man came and pushed the body inside the chamber and went to an electric panel. He pressed a switch on the panel and the doors closed. Then he pressed another switch and a horrifying sound came from the chamber.

'All move outside now' the man who operated the crematorium said.

Amaana pulled Reghu gently out of the crematorium and made him sit on a bench outside. Reghu was not normal.

After a few moments, the operator of the crematorium came outside with a memorial pot which carried the ashes of Reghu's dad.

Grandpa received the pot and went to Reghu, and handed over the ashes to him. Reghu took the pot on his hands and gazed at it. He didn't move his eyes from that. He kept on looking at it.

They all went back to home. Reghu was staring at the pot. Amaana helped him to keep the memorial pot under Dhamodhar's Photo on the wall in the living room.

After keeping the pot, Amaana took Reghu to his room. She held him by the shoulder, his body was frail. His eyes were weary.

A white Maruti 800 car came to their porch. Grandpa looked outside from the couch.

Advocate Nandha Gopal came outside from the car. He was wearing a white shirt and was carrying a file in his left hand. He walked inside the guest room. Grandpa walked bewildered to the guest room and welcomed him.

'Nandha Gopal, it's been a long time' Grandpa said.

'Yes sir' Advocate said and looked towards the new photo fixed on the wall.

'My son' Grandpa said looking to the photo on the wall.

'Yes, I know sir' Advocate said and stood up and walked towards the photo.

Grandpa followed him.

'Sir, I was the defendant in Johnson Xavier's murder case' Advocate said.

'Yes, I remember' grandpa said.

'I took that case because the police fabricated the whole thing and made him the killer' Advocate said.

'What are you talking about?' grandpa asked muddled.

'Sir, Dhinesh is innocent' Advocate said and opened the file he was carrying. He took out some photographs from it.

'Sir, these are the photos of how police got Advocate Johnson's body' Advocate said and handed over the photos. Grandpa took the photos and observed keenly. The body was inside a Jute sack. One photo was of his body, the body was full of scratches and wounds.

'He tortured the victim with knifes' Grandpa said after observing the photos.

'Now see this sir' Advocate said and hand over some other photos to grandpa.

'Which photos are these?' Grandpa asked.

'These are the photos taken when police got Dhamodhar's

body from Yeoor River' Advocate said with a pale voice.

Grandpa got struck. The body was tied up inside a jute sack exactly the same way Johnson's was. And lot of scratches were present on the body.

Grandpa started to weep after seeing the horrible condition of body.

'Sir, it is same. The killer is still out' Advocate Nandha Gopal concluded.

'Who is it, why he is doing this?' Grandpa asked weeping.

'I don't know about him sir' Nandha Gopal said and continued.

'But I know one thing, the connection between Dhamodhar and Johnson will be the next target of the killer' Advocate said and kept the photos inside the file.

Grandpa's face became red. He looked upstairs.

'You mean Reghu?' grandpa asked.

'Yes sir, but why and who, is still unknown' Nandha Gopal said.

'Gopal what should we do now?' grandpa asked helplessly.

Amaana came down from upstairs and interrupted them.

'What happened pa?' Amaana asked.

'Kuch nahi beta' grandpa tried to avoid the discussion from her.

Amaana turned to Gopalji.

'Nandha Gopal sir, Namaste' Amaana said with folded hands. Gopalji folded his hands as a reply for the Namaste.

'How is Reghu now?' Nandha Gopal asked.

'He is not speaking, he is still in shock. I think he needs a change' Amaana said.

'Yes, he needs a change from this atmosphere' grandpa said.

'If you don't mind I will take him to Punjab, my home' Amaana said.

'That would be a discomfort for your family' Nandha Gopal

said.

'I forgot to tell you she is Reghu's fiancée' grandpa said.

'Oh sorry, I don't know about it. Congrats' Nandha Gopal said with a smile on his face.

'Thank you sir.' Amaana said.

'Beta you can take him, so it would be good for him' grandpa said.

'Ok pa' Amaana said and went to kitchen.

Grandpa leaned forward to confirm that she is away from them.

'So we will get some time' grandpa said.

'Don't disclose anything about Reghu to anyone else. Just you, me and Amaana' Advocate Nandha Gopal said.

Amaana opened the door opposite to driver side of black BMW for Reghu. He was still in the shock, no reaction, he is in deep sadness. Amaana closed the door for him and went to the other side and opened the door.

'Beta, Reghu's phone? Let it be with me, I will contact you when required' grandpa said.

Amaana took Reghu's phone from her hand bag from back seat and gave it to grandpa.

'Beta, take care' grandpa said and looked at Reghu.

Reghu turned his face towards grandpa and smiled at him. Grandpa smiled at him and waved his hands as they proceeded outside.

The car started, moved slowly and they went out of the gate and disappeared. Grandpa stopped waving his hands and turned back in to house.

Advocate Nandha Gopal came through the gate inside in his white Maruthi 800. Grandpa stopped and looked back. Nandha Gopal stopped the car at the porch in front of him and got out in emergency with his laptop bag. His face was very different, he was in haste.

'Gopalji, what happened?' grandpa asked by seeing his abruptness.

'I got a lead sir' Gopalji said and got inside the house. He was very eager to tell what he had found, to someone. Gopalji switched on his laptop and kept it on the small wooden table in front of the couch. Meanwhile Gopalji took the photos of crime scene out from his laptop bag.

Grandpa got inside and sat next to Gopalji. Grandpa was feeling a bit uncomfortable on the desperate actions from Gopal.

'What you got?' grandpa asked.

'Sir, both the bodies are full of scratches and those were not of knife or any sharp object' Gopalji said.

'Then?'

'Your son was dead because of a poison from a snake bite' Gopalji said.

'What?, really' grandpa said confused.

'Yes sir, Autopsy report came and these scratches came from some animal like dogs or cats with sharp nails' Gopalji said showing the photos he brought.

'So he was killed by animals?' grandpa asked.

'Yes sir, the killer tortured him with animals and that lead to his deaths' he replied and continued by taking a photo from the diorama.

'Yes sir, look at this photo, look at his foot, that wound' Gopalji said and pointed to a 'U' shaped wound on Johnson's leg on the photo of his body and gave it to grandpa.

The opening sound of Windows OS came from laptop. Gopalji turned towards the laptop on the wooden table. He opened the My computer folder in his Desktop. Then he took Local disk(E:).

The laptop hanged. Gopalji waited for the folders to appear. Grandpa was going through the images.

Gopalji clicked on a folder called Poena Cullie and double clicked on a video inside that folder.

The video was of a dog biting a man, and the same kind of "U" shaped wound showed in that video.

'Both are similar' grandpa said after observing the images and video.

'Yes sir Snakes and dogs attacked both of them and that lead them to death' Gopalji concluded.

'Why did all this not come in Johnson's case' grandpa asked.

'Police was in hurry to close the case and they got a poor helpless guy to arrest with some witnesses' Gopalji said.

'Why did he do that?' grandpa asked and gave back the photos to Gopalji.

'It's a sign given by the killer to tell us something' Gopalji said and clicked the back button.

'What is this Gopal, Poena Cullie?' grandpa asked by seeing the different folder name.

'Yes sir that is what the killer wanted to tell us about.' Gopalji said and opened Google chrome, then typed "Poena Cullie" and pressed enter. Wikipedia popped up with an article.

"Poena Cullie, a Latin penalty of sack. Under roman law, it is a death penalty imposed on a subject who found guilty of parricide. The suspect is assorted with live animals in a sack and thrown into water after death."

CHAPTER TEN

'How are my children connected to this?' grandpa asked desperately and covered his face with his skinny hands.

'Sir, we need to find that out' Gopalji said and opened a PowerPoint file inside the Poena Cullei folder.

'Sir, killing parents is not that common. I have found all the cases that have happened in India related to parricide in recent years' Gopalji said.

Grandpa stood up and went to the diner to drink some water.

'Sir are you okay? 'Gopalji asked.

'Yeah, I'm fine' grandpa said and kept the water bottle on the table and came back to guest room where Gopal was sitting.

'Sir, look these are the cases that happened in the category of parricide in India' Gopalji said pointing towards the power point he prepared yesterday late night.

Grandpa took his reading glasses and went through the Power point.

'Awadhesh Yadav from Patna killed parents for pension in 2018' Gopalji read out loudly and continued.

'Cadell Jenson from Kerala killed parents, he has mental issues' Gopalji read out.

'Rehman from Delhi killed his parents for property' Gopalji said pointing to another slide.

'Moiz Bharmol killed his parents because of some family

dispute' Gopalji read each slides slowly for grandpa.

'Fifteen year old boy from Pune, killed parents for torturing him' Gopalji read.

'Wait Gopalji, I think I'm familiar with this case. I have heard about this before' grandpa said after reading the headline.

'It was a very famous case' Gopalji said.

Grandpa closed the powerpoint and took Google chrome and searched about the parricide in Pune. After a few moments an NDTV article came, grandpa went through it silently.

'Yes, this happened to the parents of a student in Symbiosis law college Pune' Grandpa said and looked at Gopal.

'So, what do you know about it sir?' Gopalji asked.

'Where Reghu took his LLB' he said and continued.

'Reghu's junior's parents were killed by her brother because of some dispute. Not too much but they have discussed this with me and Dhamodhar at that time'

'Will there be any connection between...?' Gopalji asked.

'We need to find it out' grandpa said and got up and walked towards his room. He was thinking something and suddenly stopped and turned back towards Gopal.

'We need to go there' grandpa said.

'Yes, I will arrange it, sir' Gopalji said.

Gopalji folded his laptop and kept inside the bag and took the photos, kept inside. He came out of the house and called the driver who was in the outhouse.

'We need to go to Pune, today evening' Gopalji said.

'Ok sir' driver agreed.

Grandpa came out of the house with a small duffle bag. He was wearing a casual blue check shirt and grey long trousers.

Advocate Nandha Gopal was waiting for him in an Audi. Grandpa looked at him.

'Are we going in this?' grandpa asked softly.

'Yes, sir' Gopalji said.

'We should keep a low profile' grandpa said and looked towards Gopalji's Maruthi 800.

Gopalji looked at his car on the porch in confusion.

'Sir, will it be able to reach our destination? It's a very old car' Gopalji said.

'It should' Grandpa said and gave his duffle bag to the driver and walked towards Maruthi. Gopalji took his backpack from Audi's trunk and went to his car.

Gopalji took keys from his backpack and put through the keyhole on the Driver side door and rotated it heavily. So the small stick-like thing came up on the door inside. Gopalji opened the door and leaned inside to pull the same little thing from the back door. He opened the back door and kept his backpack.

'Hey over here' Gopalji called the driver. Driver came to the other side to keep grandpa's bag inside.

Gopalji got inside in the driver side and leaned to the front passenger side and pulled the small stick to unlock the door. Grandpa entered inside after battling with his non flexible knees for a couple of minutes.

Gopalji started the car. Car made a special unique sound and stabilised itself. They moved out of the gate and took a diversion towards the Mumbai – Pune express highway.

'It's been three years' grandpa said.

'What sir?' Gopalji asked, looking towards grandpa.

'What are you doing, look straight and drive' grandpa said loudly.

'Okay' Gopalji said and suddenly turned his head back on

the road.

'I haven't gone out of Mumbai in three years' grandpa said looking outside through the window.

'Thanks to the suspect,' Gopalji said with a silly smile.

Grandpa turned his head to Gopalji with sharp eyes. Gopalji looked at grandpa without rotating head.

'Sorry, I didn't mean that' Gopalji said.

'Drive, drive' grandpa said.

They reached the express highway. Suddenly the wiper went on for one cycle.

'Is wiper on?' grandpa asked.

`It's automatic, sir' Gopalji said.

Grandpa looked at him for a moment and turned to the window again.

Gopalji drove at the maximum speed of his car through the last lane of the highway at fifty five kilometres per hour.

After one hour, the weather started to change, grandpa took his duffle bag from back to take his woollen cap. They reached Lonawala. Grandpa wore it and again turned his head outside.

Gopalji stopped the car after some time in front of a tea stall. Grandpa got out of the car slowly by holding the door. After getting out with the help of Gopal they went to the small stall and ordered two cups of tea.

The sunlight was weak and the sky was partially seen. The earth is wet but not raining.

Gopal and grandpa took their tea. They sipped slowly and enjoyed the cold with the hot tea. It was impossible to see long on that foggy day.

After having the tea they went back to their car and continued their journey.

CHAPTER ELEVEN

Pune

After the long non-stop journey from the tea stall they exited the express highway. The sky turned dull. They continued through the city in search of a hotel.

'Gopal, there is a hotel' grandpa said pointing towards an Oyo room.

Gopalji switched on the Yellow indicator to their left and slowly moved forward in order to find the gap between foot paths to enter the parking of the hotel. He parked the 800 in front of the Oyo hotel. Gopalji opened his door.

'Sir, you wait here let me ask whether rooms are available' Gopalji said before getting down.

Gopalji closed the door and went inside the hotel.

A lady was sitting in the reception looking at her phone and smiling.

Gopalji went to the reception and looked at her. She didn't respond. She was using earphones. Gopalji made a throat clearing sound. She noticed the sound and looked above from the phone.

Gopalji smiled at her, she took off her earphones and placed it on the table in front of her. She stood up from her seat with folded hands.

'Good evening sir, how can I help you?' Receptionist asked politely.

She was wearing a black stylior and she had a black framed

spectacles. She looked like in her early thirties.

'I need a room for a couple of days' Gopalji asked.

'Yes sir, single bed or double bed?' the receptionist asked.

'Two single bed' Gopalji said.

'Okay sir, may I have your ID please' the receptionist asked.

'Okay I will come with it, in two minutes' Gopalji said and walked out of the hotel.

Gopal went to grandpa and opened the door for him. Gopalji helped grandpa to come out. After taking grandpa out Gopalji opened the back seat to take the bags.

Gopal and grandpa got inside the hotel and went to the reception with the two bags. Gopalji took his ID and gave it to the receptionist and waited for five minutes in the lobby. Grandpa took The Hindu paper from the small table at the lobby. Receptionist called a helper using a landline phone.

After a few minutes a person came in a waistcoat and came directly to the lobby and took their bags.

'Sir, please. Your room is ready' the man said.

Gopalji and grandpa followed him to room B214. He opened the room using a key card and kept the bags at a corner and went out.

The room was great and looked like a honeymoon suit. The room had fancy lights and a table at the corner. A kettle was on the table. Gopalji went near the kettle. A tray was kept on the table near the kettle, where milk powder, coffee powder and sugar sachets are kept.

'Sir, water' waiter came in with two bottles of Fiji water.

Gopal took the bottles from the waiter and gave him a tip. Waiter thanked me and went out, closing the door.

'Sir, some coffee' Gopalji asked, holding some coffee packets.

'Yeah, no sugar' grandpa said. Grandpa was thinking of something and he was disturbed.

Gopalji went to the electric kettle and poured some water and kept it boiling. He turned to grandpa and gazed at him.

'Sir, is anything bothering you? Gopalji asked.

'Hmm, how will this be connected to my son' grandpa asked, confused.

'We will find it, sir can you explain that day when they told about the murder' Gopalji asked to make him distracted from his thinking.

'I was reading the newspaper, and I read a feature about this. As I found that college, Symbiosis law college Pune, I asked Reghu. He was having breakfast.' Grandpa said.

'Then what happened?' Gopalji asked curiously.

'He turned from the breakfast and spoke about it, about the psycho boy and the situation of a girl' grandpa said.

'That's all' Gopalji asked and switched off the kettle and poured it into two glasses.

'Yes, that's why I'm confused' grandpa said.

Gopalji made the coffee and gave it to grandpa.

'I'm tired' Gopalji said.

Sunlight came inside through the small gap between the two curtains. The fresh light struck grandpa's eyes. Gopalji was still in slumber. Grandpa opened his eyes slowly. He got up from the bed and went near the window, and moved the curtains apart. The whole room lightened up. Gopalji turned to the other side, but after a few moments he woke up.

After freshening up, they went down for breakfast provided by the hotel. Both of them were wearing cotton casuals. The breakfast had already started and had a few people.

Grandpa took three Idlis and sambar and went to a table in the right corner. Gopalji took bread toasted with butter and a watermelon juice.

'So, today?' grandpa asked.

'We are going there like brokers or like someone who wants to buy that plot' Gopalji said.

'Hmm' grandpa agreed while taking a small piece of Idli with sambar.

'So we can get maximum details from there' Gopalji said and had his last toasted bread.

They went out of the dining room and Gopalji turned towards the entrance of the hotel.

'Gopalji, one minute. I have some medicines to take' grandpa said.

Gopalji turned back and joined grandpa on his way back to the room. They went up in the lift and entered the room. Grandpa opened his duffle bag. Gopalji sat on the only chair in the room. Grandpa couldn't find his medicine box. Gopal saw grandpa finding it difficult to find his medicine box so went near to him.

'Sir, I will help you' Gopalji interrupted.

'No, I will find it' grandpa said.

Gopalji sat next to him and moved the bag to his side slowly and put his hand inside in search of the box. Gopalji's hand touched something hard and his face turned different. He pulled out the thing he touched inside the bag. It was a nine mm Luger pistol. Gopalji got terrified and left the pistol on the bed and moved away from it.

'Why sir?' Gopalji said.

'We may meet the killer on the way to tell the truth. I can't lose anyone more.'

'Sir, you too' Gopalji asked, confused.

'I don't care, I want to save my Reghu. Even if I go to jail' Grandpa said and started to cry.

'Sir, relax' Gopalji said.

'If I didn't finish him. He will hunt Reghu down' grandpa said and kept the pistol inside his bag.

Gopalji and grandpa came out of the room with his duffle bag. Gopalji didn't stop him from carrying the pistol with him.

They went out of the hotel and got inside their Maruthi 800. Grandpa kept his bag at the back seat and picked up his medicine box with him. He took his medicines for PSC.

'What was the name of that place?' grandpa asked after keeping his medicine box in his bag.

'Vijay Nagar colony' Gopalji said.

Gopalji switched on his phone for maps.

'Turn right in hundred meters' Google maps said.

Gopalji followed her and reached Vijay Nagar.

'How can we find the house?' grandpa asked by looking at the cluster of houses.

'Yes I will find it, wait inside sir.' Gopalji said and parked the car on the road side.

Gopalji went out of the car and crossed the road to a pan shop. Grandpa was looking through the glass at Gopal.

After a few minutes Gopal came back to the car and he opened the door.

'Hey, you won't like it' the pan shop keeper said loudly.

'Yeah, let me see it, thank you' Gopalji replied and got inside the car and closed the door.

'What you got?' grandpa asked.

'Yeah got the directions' Gopalji said and put the seat belt on.

'So let's go' grandpa said.

Gopal started the car and drove straight. Then took a left into a small narrow street. The street was full of houses. Gopal moved the car through the narrow street slowly.

He was looking to the right side of the street, whereas

grandpa was looking at all the houses on both sides.

'Yes, here it is' Gopal said and parked the car on the left side of the street.

Grandpa leaned towards the left to take a look at the house from the car.

The house was very old. Fully covered with brown leaves. The Front of the house is covered with tall grass. The house was not maintained for years. The walls were moss green, some parts were shattered. The house looked like a part of a horror movie.

Gopal stepped out of the car. Grandpa took the pistol and kept it in his back. They both walked towards the house slowly. They opened the gate. Suddenly a flock of birds flew up from the house. Gopalji stepped back.

'Hey, who are you?' a young man from the next door asked loudly.

Gopalji took it as a chance to get out from there so he went towards him.

'We heard this house is for sale' Gopalji said.

'Are you nuts to buy this haunting house' he asked.

Grandpa looked at Gopal. Gopal gestured to grandpa to come to him. Grandpa was still looking at the house.

'What is the problem? I know it is not maintained well.' Gopal said.

'You are from?' he asked.

'Mumbai' Gopal said.

Grandpa walked towards Gopal.

'There is a big story behind this house' he said horrified.

'Oh, what is that?' Gopal asked.

'Come inside have a seat' he said and welcomed them inside.

They entered inside the neighbour's house and sat on a brown couch. The house was very simple. Some photos were hanging on the wall opposite to the couch.

'I'm Nandha Gopal' Gopalji said and looked at grandpa.

'I'm Raj Jadhav. What happened here?' grandpa asked in curiosity.

'What is your name?' Gopalji asked purposefully to make a conversation.

'Fahad Faqir' The young man said and went to a shelf, which was on the corner of the living room. The shelf was full of Islamic antiques and albums. He took one album from the bottom. He opened it and took a folder out.

A family photo. The photo was old. A middle aged man, his wife, his young beautiful daughter and two boys.

'That boy in the red shirt is me' He said.

'Others?' Gopalji asked.

'They lived in that house' He said and sat on the wooden chair.

'We two were of the same age, we were always together. From the very beginning' he said.

CHAPTER TWELVE

Pune, 2007

POV of Fahad Faqir

The sun was very lazy and hiding behind the clouds in the morning. I was in front of the mirror styling my curly hair for fifteen minutes but still it was very disobedient to his master. That was the first day in ninth standard.

'Hey Fahad, come yaar it's getting late' He called out loudly from the street and rang his cycle bell twice.

He was ready and was waiting patiently for ten minutes outside and now he is losing his patience. I stopped working on my hair to be a good boy. I went out with my new spider man bag. I took my Hero X-sport cycle from the lone garage.

He was in his sister's ladybird, and was wearing a light blue uniform shirt and navy blue trousers. His face has changed. I didn't say anything.

We went to school every day from our KG together. We used to take the way we go to our school and all the people around were used to our journey to our school. Those days were the best, without any pressure just chilling all the time.

We reached our school, and went to the ninth class which was on the second floor of the B block. All were the same idiot classmates.

As usual I went to the back bench to conquer the

backbenchers tag of ninth class. Suddenly he pulled me back.

'What?' I asked in shock.

'It's the ninth we need to concentrate on, come let's sit in the front' he said passionately.

'What? Is that you?' I asked in confusion.

'Come on, front bench' he said.

I went with him to the dreadful first bench. I sat next to him on that bench. I smelled books on that bench. I felt uncomfortable. But he was very different and getting ready to swallow everything from the teacher.

'What happened to you?' I asked.

'Next year is our first turning point, so we need to be ready for it' he said.

'Really?' I'm still confused at his change.

He was already good in studies and always got A grades, even if he was in the last benches. Then what was he looking for? I kept on thinking of ways to get out from that book smell on the first bench.

It was ten o' clock and the second bell rang. All students got up for prayer. Then she came inside the class.

A new girl to our ninth class. She was beautiful. She was wearing a light blue Salwar Kameez with a navy blue shawl. She had a bob haircut. Her hair was straight and obedient. Her face looked so cute and her eyes were deep black and were glittering at me. Her eyes attracted my eyes like electromagnets which I learned in Physics last year. I couldn't take my eyes off of her while she walked towards her seat.

She went to the second bench. At that moment I felt he was right about the turning point and I turned back for one glance at her. A perfect turning point for my neck.

Our class teacher arrived with giant books of social science.

All stood up and greeted her with a lazy long "Ggggoooodddd mmooorninggg teeeaacherr".

"This first bench really is a hell" I murmured.

But I can sacrifice this for her beautiful eyes that always locked my eyes motionless.

'Hey come here, let us have a cute introduction from the new beautiful girl in our class' teacher looked at her and called.

"Teacher is of my taste. She is beautiful, I know" I thought.

'My name is Haifa Ajman, I'm from Wagholi' she said in her soft voice. Her voice entered inside through my ears and reached my heart.

'She is a Muslim' I said cheerfully.

The new scholar turned his face to me. His eyes were sharp. He looked at me as a police officer looking at criminals. I turned my face away from him and looked around.

"When will this show be over?" I thought.

'How much?' I asked him as he got the paper from the teacher and got back to his seat.

He showed me his paper with a gloomy face.

'What forty seven on fifty! This is bad' I said, amazed.

'I lost two marks on this question' he said.

'Still you are not satisfied, do you want to sit on the teacher's table for those two marks?' I asked.

'Fahad' teacher called out loudly.

I looked at her face. It was not that good, so I stood up and went to her. I took the paper from her table as it was thrown before I reached. I didn't look at my marks, from her reaction itself I understood its low. I came back to my seat.

'Hey, how much did you get?' he asked in great enthusiasm.

I showed him the paper. He took it from my hands and opened it.

'Not bad you got forty' he said in joy.

I got confused, 'What?' I asked.

He gave me the paper back and I looked at my marks. "It's forty on fifty, my highest score in life" my heart jumped with excitement.

'So now tell, the first benches always had these kinds of advantages' he said.

"Really it was not the first bench, it's her" I thought.

I turned my head towards her. She was buried in her paper looking very hard. She slowly took her eyes away from her paper and looked at me.

She asked how much I got by a hand gesture.

I showed four fingers in my right hand and gave a silly smile. She also smiled at my marks.

I asked about her score by the same gesture she showed me. Her face went dark. She didn't respond, she went back to her paper as if she was looking for some treasure.

All students were busy with their papers, some were chatting, some girls are making some way to steal more marks and I was fully engaged in looking at her and dreaming.

One hour went away with me looking at her face, somehow the scholar was busy finding a way to steal the two marks he lost on Harappan civilization.

Teacher went out of the class after the bell. All moved from their places and I was still busy looking at her.

'Fahad, you have done enough damage to her face' Scholar said.

He pulled me out. I left the class and waited outside on the veranda. He told me about the adventurous mark hunt he has done to get those two marks.

She folded her paper and kept it inside her bag and came out of the class, she was with her friends, she crossed me and in that moment she looked at my eyes, it was shining.

'You haven't seen girls before?' the scholar asked, feeling irritated by my new crush.

'Yes I have but not her' I said in a romantic accent.

'Disgusting' he said.

'You will not understand love, It is the beat of the earth' I said posing like SRK looking to the sky with my hands wide open.

'Don't go so far, she will not love you' he said.

She returned back to the veranda with her friends. I gazed at her eyes. She went to the class going past me again. This time she didn't look.

She entered the class and suddenly stopped. She turned back and walked towards me. Scholar's eyes got wide open.

'Is she coming towards us?' he whispered.

She came near me. A beautiful aroma spread all around us. She stood next to me by supporting on the half wall of the veranda. She looked into my eyes.

'You got forty, so you are intelligent, and you?' she said smiling and looked at him.

"Damn, if he tells his mark I'm finished" I thought.

'He got thirty eight' I said and looked at him and begged to save my face by giving a pleading look.

He didn't say a word and agreed by shaking his head.

'I only got thirty five, in one question in the essay, I got really confused' she said with regret.

'It's not a big deal, next time we can crack it. If you need any help on studies you can ask me' I said with leniency.

'You both are always together?' she asked, looking at both of us.

'Yeah, we are neighbours, friends first' he said.

'Wow, you guys are lucky, having such great company. I was alone for a long time, but now I have some friends' she said desperately.

'Oh, no worry, you can join us. We are looking for a new member' I said with a huge smile on my face and turned to him for approval.

His face was not that clear. I turned my face back to her cute little face.

She smiled at us.

'So see you, bye' she said and turned.

'Bye, Fa' I shortened her name. She noticed it and smiled at me and went inside, my eyes followed her.

'Faaaa, what was that?' He asked in a disgusted way.

I winked at him and got inside the class for the next tedious forty minutes.

The scholar was always in his studies, and my eyes were always on her. Both our eyes were targeted on the goals we need to achieve.

'She is so beautiful, I want to hug her right now' I said looking at her cute smile.

Her eyes moved from the teacher to me.

'Oh shit' I said and rolled my eyes away.

'What? scholar got distracted from his studies?'

'Nothing, she looked at me' I said in great joy.

'She has the right to look around, it's not because you are sitting here' he said in a plain voice.

'Politics is going on right, good. Concentrate in the class, ok' I said and turned his face back to the teacher with my hands.

She became very close to me, she used to come to me for

clear doubts. I would ask those to the scholar and clear it afterwards to her. We became good friends. We became a trio on our morning and evening cycle rides. Those days were filled with joy and happiness.

'Bro, I need your help' I said to him, he was reading a magazine.

'What help?' he asked.

'I need to score high marks, please teach me' I said.

'Oh now you want high marks, Why?' he said in a teasing tone looking at me.

'I want to keep up my grades and to show that I'm good at studies even in front of her' I said.

'Even though it is for her, at least you want to learn, good!! I will help you' he said and went back to reading the magazine.

'What are you reading? VO...GUE... Is it for an exam?' I asked, looking at the magazine he was reading.

'No yaar, it's just for pleasure' he said.

'Oh so you do things for pleasure too?' I asked.

'I'm focused in the class in order to reduce work at home, so I can do stuffs I like as well as teach some people who want to score high marks for their crush' he said without eye contact.

I sneered at him. He smirked at me.

'Hey, from tomorrow no evening games' he said.

'What, you are already not coming and now you restrict me?' I asked, frustrated.

'Do you want to impress her?' he asked boldly.

'Yeah, but' I said hesitantly.

'So my rules' he said with authority.

'Okay' I said in dissatisfaction.

'You read this, this will definitely come for the exam' my new teacher gave me a tip about thermodynamics.

'Oh' I exclaimed. 'This is a big derivation, I can't gulp it' I said after seeing the long derivation in his notebook.

'Faaaa' he said and looked at me.

'Yeah, I will try' I said in a low voice.

'Write it one time in your book then read it one time. Then close the book and write' he said confidently.

'That's it?' I asked and took my rough note and started writing.

'Fahad' he called out loudly.

'Yeah coming' I said.

'Ready for the last exam?' he asked when I came out with my cycle to the narrow road in front of my house.

'Yeah, somehow I'm ready. But I am really waiting for the Christmas celebrations' I said with great happiness.

'Why?' he asked, noticing the glow in my face.

We started our ride to school through the narrow road. The sky was bright and clear.

'I will tell her about my love for her' I said.

'Tomorrow?' he asked, confused and his eyes became broad.

'Yeah, it's been six months that I'm in love. We need to settle this' I said firmly.

'Oh, what do you need to settle?' he asked and laughed at me.

'Hey, she is coming, act naturally' I said after seeing her coming on her cycle towards us in the junction where we meet every day.

She was a little tense, her face was not that charming that day. She came and joined us.

'Hey what happened? You seem tensed' I asked politely.

'I'm afraid for this last exam, those derivations' she said. Her voice was low.

'Exams are in the afternoon, I will help you make those easy. I have some tricks' I said.

The new teacher sharply looked at me. That eye contact was so terrible. We reached the school and I parked my X-sport in the empty cycle shed. Nobody came to the school in the morning because the exams were in the afternoon. We were called by Haifa to come early for some final preparation.

We went to our class, it was a hollow room and was in perfect silence. I went to the first bench together with him. He took his books out and started his work of swallowing paragraphs, derivations, even the problems.

"Wow nobody is here, I can be with her all day" I thought in my mind.

She put her bag on the girl's side and came towards me with her notebook. The rough note was perfectly covered with brown paper and a Barbie label on it.

"She was looking as beautiful as that beautiful Barbie girl on the label" I thought.

'Tell me and teach me your tricks' she said in a silly way and sat next to me on the first bench.

The scholar gave me a glance. I didn't consider him as a threat to our love. I moved closer to her.

'Which all derivations are creating issues for you, I want to see them right now' I shouted like a teacher.

She smiled at my dialogue. Her eyes are so close to my eyes. She looked at the scholar who was busy with his thermodynamics. She moved her hair aside, it fondled my

face and it was so smooth and silky. Her Kasturi savour spread all over. I inhaled her fragrance. She looked again in my eyes. Her eyes were glittering, filled with intense love.
'This is the most cruel one, kill him first' she said to me. Suddenly I moved back to her voice.
"Thanks Mr. Scholar" I thought.
We learned together sitting closer till the first alien came inside the class for the exam. She slowly moved away from me and went back to her seat. If this type of learning is followed everywhere, boys will score an A plus in all the subjects, even in Mathematics.

CHAPTER THIRTEEN

POV of Fahad Faqir

I opened my small wardrobe, looking for my new red long sleeve shirt. I had saved it for this day since two months. I opened the transparent cover and took it out. The fragrance of modish spread inside the room. I wore it and looked in the mirror, rolled up the sleeves and started working on my hair.

That day, I didn't hear my friend's voice loud, because I woke up at six to get ready. I took my cycle out of my garage and waited on the steps for him to arrive with his. I rehearsed in a low voice what I was going to tell her that day.

As usual he wore a simple casual shirt and came in front of my house. Without even looking he started his daily routine.

'Hey Fahaa...' he called out loudly and stopped when he noticed me sitting ready to go.

'Really, you are ready today on time?' he asked.

'Yeah actually five minutes early' I said proudly.

'Hmm, let's go. There is a chance of rain today' he said in a joking tone. I looked at the bright sky.

I took my cycle out and started our journey to school for the Christmas celebration.

'So today you will tell her right' he said.

'Yes' I said confidently.

'Will she accept it? I don't think she will' he said.

'Oh negative vibes, she will. Are you jealous?' I said looking at him.

'Jealous, not at all, but I will miss your company' he said sadly.

'Oh, that was the thing. She is different and you are different' I said looking at his gloomy eyes. We reached the junction where she used to join us every day. We stopped our journey for her to reach. I started looking for her at the end of the road that I could see. We stepped down from our cycles.

'Here she is' he said when she appeared at the end of the road. I turned to look at her.

She was wearing a red long skirt and a glowing white shirt. She reached near us. We got back on the cycles and started to ride. She joined us. She was looking so cute in that dress. The white shirt and red long skirt with a bow on it.

'You are looking so beautiful' I complimented.

'Thanks, don't you want to say anything?' she asked and looked at the scholar who was concentrating on the road.

He turned to her and smiled and looked at me.

'You both are in the same colour, wow match- match' he said.

It was the first supportive dialogue from him for my love. She looked at me and said.

'We are in red, you look handsome in red' she said.

"So I'm handsome" I thought.

We reached school. In the gate our principal was standing in Santa Claus costume and was giving toffees to every student. We also got toffees, it was one of my favourite "Lacto-King". It was a popular toffee at that time. Still it is my favourite. A hard caramel flavoured sweet wrapped with golden cover. It will remain in your mouth for several minutes.

We went inside our class after parking our cycles. Our class was decorated by stars and merry glittering balls. Our teacher was instructing boys to decorate the class.

After decorating the class, the teacher went out. I went near her, she was with her friends.

'I....' I started to tell her. She interrupted me and said.

'I want to tell you something, after this can we meet under grandpa, bring him too' she said.

"Grandpa" it's an old banyan tree at our school. The tree was very huge and I used to go there for some calm and peace. Grandpa gives positive vibes to all. I was also about to fix that place for our meeting, but she booked it first.

'You were about to tell something, what was that?' she asked.

'I will tell you later' I said and turned around.

Teacher came inside the class with a box. And kept the box on her table. She opened it. Everyone was looking at the huge box.

It was a creamed marble cake. Everyone went near it and the teacher told everyone to sing a Christmas song.

We wish you a merry Christmas
We wish you a merry Christmas
We wish you a merry Christmas
And a happy new year.
We wish you a merry Christmas
We wish you a merry Christmas
We wish you a merry Christmas
And a happy new year.

Teacher cut the cake into several pieces and started giving it to all of her students. All were happy. I was happier that she called me to tell me something in private and also the happiness of the delicious marble cake with vanilla cream.

'She wanted to tell me something, you should also come with me' I said to him while having a large bite of a cake piece.

'Why me?' he asked.

'You need to hear what she says' I said.

While having another bite I looked at her. She looked back at me and smiled.

It's noon and the sunlight was very strong, still it felt cool under our grandpa. I was a little tense and was standing looking at the infinite blue sky. He was sitting on one of the large roots and doing something with stones. Banyan leaves were falling down in the light breeze.

She walked slowly towards us. He stood up from the root and put down the stones he was holding. Her eyes were glittering in the sunlight. She came near me and smiled at me.

She turned me around with her soft hands by holding my shoulders and turned my back towards her.

'I love your friend, I want to be with him. Please tell him' she said at my back and giggled.

One yellow leaf fell slowly in front of me. I heard the sound of that leaf touching the ground.

I got really confused. "She was in love with him, she didn't even talk to him. She was coming to me for him" my mind got freaked, but I kept my silence. She just became friends with me for him, the Scholar.

"So when she was sitting with me her eyes were on him, I was just a......" I just thought of previous days when we were together.

All went silent, he was also totally confused. He raised his face and looked at me. My face was blank, no emotions. He cleared his voice.

"What he said was right, she won't love me. Did he know about this before?" my mind got fully messed up.

'I didn't even think of you Haifa and I will not be a good partner for you. I can't give you a positive answer' he said and cleared from the scene.

She turned me back to her. I saw her face, it was pale and broken. I couldn't tell her anything, I was speechless. She turned back and went away from me. My eyes got blurred, they were filled with tears. I went near the grandpa and sat down. I couldn't keep my eyes clear. I kept my face down and covered.

'Hey, come let's go' he said by holding me on the shoulder.

'I didn't expect this, you won' I said and raised my face.

'Don't worry man. I'm always with you. She doesn't deserve you' he said, holding my shoulder.

'Why didn't you accept her love? She is beautiful and good' I asked him.

'I don't know I can't love her' he said and got up.

'Come on Mr. Romeo 'he said and pulled me up.

I went close to him and I hugged him. Again my eyes filled with tears, this time it was not for her, it's for his endless company and support.

"Where is he, why is he not getting out at all? It's been two days. Did he stop playing cricket too? Something serious is going on" I thought while I'm holding my medium size local cricket bat with the MRF logo. I told everyone that it is an original and Sachin Tendulkar is using the same bat for his matches. Really it is only one fifty rupees. But that secret will end with me and my dad.

I went to his house to find what happened to him. I parked

my cycle in front of his house and went inside. I kept my bat on the porch and got inside the house.

'Aunty, where is he?' I asked his mother who was busy preparing chapatis for dinner.

She was wearing an apron and her daughter was helping her out with frying chapattis.

'He is here, check in his room' mother said. I walked out of the kitchen and walked towards the bedroom. He and his sister were in the same room. The door was closed but not locked. I opened it without knocking.

He was sitting in front of the mirror, he didn't look at me. He was still staring at the mirror. I can only see one side because I'm standing at the door.

'Hey man, why are you not coming for cricket, have you seen my new MRF bat that Sachin Tendulkar also has' I asked with pride, whenever I tell that last portion I feel guilty inside, still I continue to tell it to everyone.

'I don't want to play' he said.

'You told me that you will be with me forever' I told him to make him feel uncomfortable.

He turned to me. He had applied black eye liner. The lines were so perfect and his eyes were so attractive. My face changed when I saw his face. I pursed my lips inside to avoid laughing at him. Then I broke my mouth open and laughed pointing to his face.

Now his face changed to sneer. I stopped laughing slowly as I saw his face changing rapidly.

'What happened?' I asked by stopping my laugh.

'Nothing, just for pass time' he said and turned back to the mirror.

I got inside the room and sat behind him on the bed. Now we both are in the reflection of the mirror.

'If you were a girl, I would have proposed to you' I said to make him more frustrated.

Really he was looking so beautiful, just by putting on an eye liner. His face changed entirely to a beautiful lady's face. If he had a little more hair, I would have instantly fallen in love with him.

But he looked down, I didn't get the reaction I was looking for. I understood that he was upset. I understood something is really going on in his mind.

I went near him, and held his shoulders.

'What happened my boy?' I asked.

'Nothing' he said, he laid down his head on my right hand and looked at the mirror.

His eyes started glittering, filled with tears.

"Why is he crying? Is it because I teased him or for something else" I thought.

'I don't know what is happening to me. I'm changing' he said in pain.

'What are you talking about?' I asked, looking at him through the mirror.

He went silent and closed his eyes. I brushed his soft long hair with my left hand to cheer him up. He opened his eyes and looked at my face in the mirror.

'I want to live like a girl' he said.

'What?' I took my hand from his shoulders in shock.

He turned to me, when I suddenly made that movement.

'I don't know why. These things attract me, I want to live like a girl' he said.

I got really confused, a fourteen year old boy is not much grown to give a mature reply for that. I went silent for a moment. I felt uncomfortable and went outside of his room without telling anything.

The next day, I didn't wait for his daily reminder for school. I went without him to school. I felt bad for him, I don't know why I did that to him. Society made me act like a moron those days. I went to the back bench to avoid his company completely. Today I feel ashamed for what I did that day.

The girl inside him started to conquer him completely. Other students also started realising his change. His appearance, walk, even his talking has changed a lot.

Everyone started noticing his new changes and rumours started taking rounds from every corner. I felt very bad whenever I heard about him.

His parents got to know about the gossip. They started trying to change him back to being a boy.

His family started hating him, he really became alone. At last, he was sent to Swami Kalyan Samarthan who was famous for Psychological counselling.

The days without seeing him were worse for me. That made me realise his importance in my life. I understood my mistake of leaving him alone in that situation.

He returned from the Swami after two weeks. I went to see him. He was sitting alone in his room. He hasn't spoken to anyone after coming back home. His house was in grave silence.

I went inside his room. He was sitting on his bed looking outside through the small window. The room was dark, only a little light came from a small window. He felt my presence, but didn't respond.

'Hey' I called out from the door.

He didn't respond.

I went near and sat next to him. I also looked out through

the small window.

'Sorry' I said in a plain voice.

He didn't respond to my apology. We both looked out through the small window for a few minutes.

After some time he laid his head on my shoulder. He was weeping. I felt guilty, I was also among them who made him suffer. He wiped his face with his hands.

'What happened?' I asked.

'They counselled me first with their sharp voice, then they used their power to abuse to change me' he said in pain. His voice was breaking and was very low. He was fully drained and broken.

'Did they hurt you?' I asked him.

'I started acting like a man for my life' he said.

CHAPTER FOURTEEN

POV of Fahad Faqir's friend

Swami Kalyan Samarthan Ashram.

I went there half hearted, my parents compelled me to go for the counselling. They cannot accept a transgender in their family.

I reached the Ashram. It was a calm and quiet place. The place was a green canvas and had a great positivity. They took me inside and my family disappeared from my sight. I felt like I'm in safe hands. The treat they provided was so pleasant.

I went inside my room and arranged everything. The moody cool ambience and the old fashioned clean white bed called me towards it. I went near the bed and touched the white clean bed sheet. It was cold. My eyes gave a signal to my brain to fall on it. After a long time, I got a good sound sleep.

Knock! Knock! I heard the sound on my door. It was polite but disturbed my sleep. I woke up refreshed and went slowly to my door. The room was dark like on a rainy day.

The antique locking of the door was new for me. I opened the door, the bright light came and struck my retina. I closed my eyes. I felt a shadow coming in front of my eyes. I opened my eyes slowly and saw him.

Swami Kalyan Samarthan, he had a long black beard. His eyes were glowing and his dress was shining in the bright light. I felt divinity around me.

He extended his right hand towards me, the fingers were decorated with golden rings with precious stones. My eyes caught the rings for a moment. My left hand went without any hesitation towards him.

I walked with him through a green grassed path. All the steps I made on the fresh green grass made me feel better and better.

Swamiji was talking about something but I couldn't concentrate on it. He opened the door and went inside holding me. The same darkness that I was enjoying inside my room came again. The room had two chairs which were very old. Swamiji was fully calm, he offered me a chair. I made myself comfortable, he also took the seat. The doors then closed.

Swamiji welcomed me to the ashram. And gave me a brief description about what I have to do in the coming days. Yoga in the morning, Counselling, discussions, prayer and sleep.

When he completed his conversation the doors opened. The bright light came inside. I moved out of the room and targeted my room to complete my sleep.

While going to my room I saw a tired girl walking half asleep through the grass. Her eyes were half closed and gloomy. Her shoulders were down. I looked at her. She raised her eyes up a little. Those eyes were telling me something about my coming days, but at that moment I couldn't understand it.

I went to continue my sleep. The ambiance inside my room was made for a sound sleep.

The sound of music inside my room, it was a pleasant one, slowly I got up from the bed. It was morning six. My eyes were so fresh. The music stopped after a few minutes.

I washed my face and went to the lawn where all the people were present for yoga. Some foreigners, old retired uncles and me. I looked for the girl I saw yesterday, but she was not there. All had a happy face and seemed so excited for the yoga.

One instructor came in white kurta and loose pyjamas. She came near the statue of an old man that looked like a Rishi. She sat crossing legs. Everyone faced her and crossed their legs. Yoga started with some breathing exercises.

The yoga went on for an hour and ended with Shavasana. All went out of the lawn. I went to the statue of the old rishi enthusiastically. The statue was of Sushruta, an ancient Indian physician, who was the son of Vishvamitra in Mahabharata. The details about the statue were engraved on the stone where the statue was kept.

'Hello' a person called me from the veranda.

I turned around and looked at him.

'Come, time for counselling' he said very softly.

I went with him to the same room where I went yesterday. Swamiji was sitting and was waiting for me. I felt guilty for making him wait. I took my seat in front of him. Swamiji was really cool. I saw a special brightness on his face. His face was glowing.

'Namaste beta' Swamiji said by folding his hands.

'Namaste Swamiji' I said and folded my hands too.

'What is your problem beta? Why are you making your parents sad?' Swamiji asked politely.

'I don't have any problem. My parents, classmates, this society and you have the problem' I said in order to defend myself.

Swamiji didn't feel good with my reply. His face changed. He looked behind me in the dark. His eyes were sharp.

My head turned in the direction of his eyes. A man

appeared from the darkness, he had a muscular body. I was startled. He came near me. My heart started beating fast. "What is he going to do?" I thought. I looked at Swamiji.
He slightly moved his head and gave a signal to the goon who was now standing right behind me. He held my long hair and pulled it back harshly. I held his hand with my two hands as a reflex.
He started pulling my hair upwards. I started feeling pain in my neck and head. I started screaming. But nothing stopped, I got elevated from the chair and my body got suspended in the air, against the gravitational law.
I was screaming not for help, because of the intense pain. I felt like my skin was separating from my skull. My eyes started to flow. I got exhausted, I tried to touch the ground with my foot, but couldn't. The pain began to take over me. My body was sweating a lot. I felt like I was losing my soul. After a moment I went silent, I started feeling less pain. And I blacked out.

I opened my eyes, I had pain in my head. I was lying under a shower. I was alone. I tried to get up by supporting the floor with my hand. I looked down and the floor was red, I took my hands off. It was my blood and it came from my neck. I felt a burn at the back of my head. Somehow I got up from the floor. My dress was blood red. I was feeling drowsy. I washed the blood off my body and tried to get out of the bathroom.
I opened the door which was not locked. He was standing right outside the bathroom. I stepped back. But he held my hands firmly and pulled me out of the bathroom. He took me back to Swamiji. That same room where I blacked out. One day was over. No yoga, no food.

'How are you feeling now? Is all our problems gone or is it still there?' Swamiji asked.

I was tired but my heart was still strong.

'You cannot finish your problem by killing me, it's your disability' I said in a bold voice.

"I don't know why I said that to him"

This time he didn't show any signals to the goon. He stood up from his chair with rage. He came near me and held my two hands. I protested by pulling my hands away. The goon came and held my hands and gave it to Swamiji. He held my hands and raised it up.

The goon pulled my dress off. I felt naked, I pulled my hands off to cover my body. I was just in my underpants. I tried to cover my body. He pulled my hands up again. This time it was strong.

The goon came with a stool and placed it in front of me. He raised me to the stool. I was confused about what they are going to do now. Swami pulled my hands up and tied it to the rope attached from the roof.

Again my eyes started flowing, I couldn't resist them. The women inside me made my eyes flow. After tying my hands both went away.

Then I tried to get down from the stool but my foot didn't touch the floor. My hands started stretching out. My muscles were burning. I jumped back to the stool. I was done, I couldn't move. I have to stand until my hands are free.

'Stay there until you change back to what your body is' He said in anger and went out of the room. The goon went towards the dark. I looked around. I couldn't see anything.

My body was weak, I didn't have food or water for one day. I stood there alone.

Hours passed. My muscles started burning. My joints got

strained. My eyes started drooping. Nobody attended to me.

I wanted to urinate. I screamed for someone. Nobody came. I couldn't control it. I urinated standing. I stood on that small stool. It became darker. I couldn't sleep.

My legs were immobilized. Time passed on. My heart started getting weaker. All hope in life was gone. They will kill me, if I protest. My confidence, boldness and everything burned away. My heart and mind clouded with dismay.

A small light came from a small window. The light ray touched my right eye. I opened my eyes in great pain. I was half dead already. The door opened. I took a deep breath, He came inside and stood in front of me.

I looked at him with my weak eyes. His face was arrogant.

'How is it now? All our problems are gone? Got a lot of time to think about it?' he said.

I was no longer powerful to protest, my body and mind were dead.

'I want to live, please don't kill me' I pleaded in pain.

'Okay that is good' he said.

He raised my head up with his right hand. I looked at his face.

'So you are a man, you have to be a man, or otherwise we will meet again' he said and took off his hand. My head fell down. I was not having the energy to keep my head up.

I started acting like a man, because I didn't want to see that place anymore.

CHAPTER FIFTEEN

POV of Fahad Faqir

He was weeping while telling his worst days there at the ashram. I understood how much torture he went through. I felt guilty for what I have done to him before. I was one among them.

He laid his head slowly on my shoulder, but his eyes were still on that light coming through the small window. I went quiet.

'I love you' he said in a low voice. I smiled and brushed his hair slowly.

'Oww, it's still painful' he said.

I took my hands off suddenly.

"What he needs is some support, even the family is against him. Sorry not 'him' it's 'her'"

I thought while she was lying on my shoulder. She didn't speak a word, we sat there for a while.

'Hey, tu nikal abhi' her dad came inside the room and shouted. He was exasperated. I got scared. We both stood up and looked at him.

'You did this all to my child, get out of here now' he said, I was shocked.

I didn't respond to him, so I went out of the room and looked back. "Once it was a happy family, now it is the worst" I thought and walked back to my house. "Why did he make me responsible for this?" I was totally confused and hurt.

I heard loud noises from her house. "He was also torturing her, please don't kill her, Allah" I prayed inside.

I went inside my house. I didn't feel good. I really wanted to see her, but couldn't. I couldn't sleep well. Whenever I closed my eyes, her face and our past memories would appear. The happy days we had.

Time went on, I managed to lie on the bed till morning. I got up when the first ray got inside my room. I wanted to meet her, I want to talk to her and apologize for what I had done before.

I opened the front door. There was a large squad of police on our lane, I got confused. Suddenly my mother pulled me inside by holding my hands. I didn't understand anything.

"Why are there police in our colony? What happened?"

I really got scared. My mother looked at me. Her eyes were heavy.

'Go inside and forget him' she said.

'What happened?' I asked.

'His father and mother are dead' she said.

'What?' I asked.

'Your friend killed them, he is a psycho' she said.

I didn't reply. I went inside my room. I looked in the mirror. "How can she do that? No she won't do that" I thought.

I went out to see what was going on. Police were there doing their investigation about the murder. I didn't find her anywhere. Policemen were roaming around, some were in discussion and some were sitting inside their jeep. I went back home.

I switched on the TV and switched to a local news channel. The breaking news was about the murder. I watched to understand what happened after I left her house.

She was displayed as a psycho. They didn't give any information about the counselling or her transformation. They pictured him as a freak that killed his parents for pleasure.

After a moment, they showed live from the house.

'Now the police have arrived at the crime spot for first level investigation with the main suspect' news reporter said.

I went out again to find out if it's live. Then I found a crowd in front of her house. I walked towards her house. I waited there for the police to come out. They were rushing inside the house.

I waited outside in the sun for thirty minutes, people started leaving as the sun was so strong.

Police came out. Crowd became a little weird. I searched for her. She was covered by a group of police men. They were pulling her to the police van. She went inside, she was handcuffed. She looked out.

She saw me, I looked at her. Her face was pessimistic. She was broke. I didn't find guilt in her eyes. They went with her.

I was gloomy, I was confused. But all the evidence went against her. She was sent for five year in the juvenile detention centre. There was an eyewitness, which was the main evidence against her.

After that day, I didn't see her. Still I remember her whenever I see this house.

POV of Third person

'So where is the elder sister? What happened to her' grandpa asked.

Fahad raised his face and looked at the old man.

'We didn't go behind them. After that day neither me or my family saw them. He would have been released from the detention, but never came back here' Fahad said.

Grandpa and Gopalji were silent. Three of them didn't make eye contact with each other.

Suddenly Gopalji asked with curiosity.

'Who was that eye witness?'

Fahad looked at Gopalji with a sneer on his face.

'He is always curious' grandpa said politely.

'I didn't see him but I know his address' Fahad said.

A lady came from the kitchen to the living room with coffee. Grandpa and Gopalji took the coffee cups.

'This is my wife, Haifa' Fahad said.

Gopalji looked at her once and looked back at Fahad's face with confusion. Fahad winked back at Gopalji and smiled.

'I married her' Fahad said.

Gopalji and grandpa smiled at them.

After having the coffee, Fahad went inside for the details of the eyewitness.

'We heard your story' Gopalji said to her.

'Sir, I know where she is?' Haifa said.

'You know?' grandpa asked.

'Her parents were killed in front of her and she was shocked, after that her mental state was not stable' Haifa said and took the tray with the empty coffee cups.

'So is she in any metal hospital?' Gopalji asked.

'She is not mental, her mind is not stable. She is at Dr.

Benjamin's Psychological centre' she said and looked behind for Fahad.

'Thank you' grandpa said.

Few moments later Fahad came out of the room. His face was not pleasant.

'Sir I couldn't find it, I think I missed it' Fahad said.

Haifa went inside with the coffee glasses.

'Ok beta, no problem' grandpa said and moved slowly towards the door. Grandpa held the door and went out of the house.

The sky became a bit dark again. It was grey. The sky was about to cry. They rushed towards the car.

Both got inside the car and looked at each other.

'Why did he hide the information from us?' Gopalji asked.

'He knows that we will bring danger to them' grandpa said and looked forward.

'The story will not be over without her,' grandpa said looking at the rain drops on the front glass.

Gopalji drove the car out of the colony.

'Stop' grandpa said and hit gently on the dashboard.

Gopalji stopped the car immediately and looked at grandpa 'What happened sir? Did you forget anything?' Gopalji asked.

'We need to come back here tonight, we need to check the house' grandpa said.

#

It was an Amavasya. The sky was fully dark. Gopalji drove slowly through the colony, nobody was outside. When they reached near the house grandpa signalled to shut the head lamps. Gopalji switched off the head lamps and the narrow lane became invisible. Gopalji managed to move the car slowly towards the house and stopped gently.

They got out of the car and looked around to check whether

anyone was looking at them. Gopalji and grandpa walked slowly through the gate of the old house. There was a small path towards the back of the house which did not have long grass.

'Look Gopal, how did this track appear here if no one was using it this way, this is why I came here' grandpa Whispered.

Gopalji was not in a condition to think like grandpa, he was a little terrified. Grandpa followed the grassless path and went slowly to the back side of the house. His eyes were sharp and were moving rapidly all around.

Meanwhile Gopalji was concentrating on the frightening darkness. He was hoping he would be encountered from any angle.

Grandpa reached the back door of the house and looked for Gopalji, who was busy with his myths and childhood stories.

Grandpa hissed at Gopalji. Gopalji turned towards the source of the sound with a martial arts block.

Grandpa shook his head looking at Gopalji. Gopalji slowly brought his hands down and dashed towards grandpa.

They both looked at the back door. It was closed and chained with a rusty lock. They went near the door. Grandpa took the lock in his shivering hands.

Gopalji turned around in search of a stone. He brought a sharp stone from that grassy plot. Gopalji raised the stone high to strike on the lock. Suddenly grandpa blocked him by holding his hands. Gopalji looked grandpa for an explanation. Grandpa took off his sweater and gestured to wrap the stone with it.

Gopalji brought back the stone to sea level. Grandpa wrapped it and gave it back to Gopalji.

He raised it again and hit hard on the lock. The lock and

chain moved outwards from the door and hit the back of the door. But they stayed connected.

Gopalji went for the second strike. The lock remained firm. They went again and again. Each time they hit, the lock loosen. On the seventh time an additional sound came from the lock.

Grandpa held the lock and pulled the lock apart. Gopalji threw the stone with the sweater away and held the chains and moved it outward.

'Where is my sweater?' grandpa whispered.

Gopalji looked around to find where he threw the stone. But it disappeared into the grass. Grandpa looked at Gopal with his sharp eyes.

'It's an evidence for our presence, Go and find it' grandpa said in a low voice.

Gopalji went away from grandpa to find the sweater.

Grandpa slowly opened the old double door. And peeked inside. It was inky inside. Grandpa opened the door fully. The doors were silent.

Grandpa confirmed that this house is used by someone frequently. Grandpa stepped inside. Everything was immersed in darkness. Gopalji entered the house after taking the sweater. He also couldn't see anything. Both of them looked around.

'Sir, look there' Gopalji said.

Grandpa looked towards his sound.

'What? I can't even see you' grandpa said.

'There is a small red light, the house has power' Gopalji said.

'Really, then search for a switch' grandpa said.

Gopalji started to touch through the walls.

'The roofs are leaking, the walls are wet, sir' Gopalji said.

'Are you here to buy this house?' grandpa asked.

'I got one switch' Gopalji said with excitement.
'Put it on' grandpa said curiously.
Gopalji switched on. The light flickered two times. Few seconds later it lightened the whole room.
They both looked around shocked and went motionless.

CHAPTER SIXTEEN

Dogs started barking at them. Gopalji moved back. The house was like hell. The floors had streams of blood. Blood stained walls.

Dogs were so furious, they kept on barking. They were caged. The hunger for flesh was reflected in their bark.

'This is a torture room' grandpa said.

'Sir, let's get out of here. It's not safe here' Gopalji said and moved slowly towards the door.

Grandpa looked around for evidence that connected with his son. He went inside the room.

He entered a bedroom which seemed abandoned for years, he went to the bathroom attached to it. The door was closed. Grandpa opened the door using his sweater.

It was dark inside the toilet. He switched on the light. The light was flickering. He went inside it. Spider webs were all around. Grandpa moved them with his hands and looked around. Some papers were kept at the left corner behind a small square mirror. He went near the mirror and slowly took the rectangular paper pieces with his left hand.

It was just black and white hard papers. Grandpa rotated them to the partial light. He saw the picture of Johnson. He switched the first picture to his right hand. Dhamodhar's picture was the second.

Grandpa closed his eyes and switched the photo to his right hand. The next was Reghu's. Grandpa's eyes filled with tears.

He put the pictures back and walked back to Gopal broke down in tears.

'Sir, what happened?' Gopalji asked.

'My grandson is the next victim' Grandpa said and went out of the house.

Grandpa turned back to Gopal and said.

'Please make sure everything is back at its place. We don't want him to know about our visit'

Gopalji switched off the lights and closed the door. Grandpa went back to the car. His head was down.

Gopalji drove the car back to the hotel. Grandpa didn't say a word. He went directly to his bed.

'Gopalji' grandpa called him by patting his shoulders.

He woke up and looked at him.

'We need to go, I need to save my grandson' grandpa said.

Gopalji got out of his bed and freshened up. He got ready within a few minutes and they vacated the hotel as soon as they could.

'Sir, where are we heading to?' Gopalji asked looking grandpa.

'Dr. Benjamin's Psychological centre, Matheran' grandpa said.

Grandpa gave his phone with the map to Gopalji. He took a look at the map sitting inside the car and gave back the phone.

Gopalji started the engine and moved out of the hotel. They went through the vacant streets towards the high way.

The sun was still sleeping. They entered the long highway. Grandpa looked forward, hardly blinking. Gopalji was a little tired. He couldn't complete his sleep last night.

They travelled a hundred kilometres through the highway. Grandpa read a diversion board out loud.

'Matheran thirty seven kilometres' grandpa said.

Gopalji turned the car to the left and exited the highway. The roads changed from straight to a little steep and curvy. They stopped for a restroom at a gas station. They had their breakfast. Little foggy and cold. The ray from the sun reflected from the car parked outside.

Gopalji went out and checked the route towards their destination. Grandpa came out of the hotel after paying. They took the car and continued their journey.

The nature and the landscape were too good and refreshing, but they were not in the mood to enjoy it. They went through the steep roads and a couple of sharp turns. Maruthi 800 went slowly on the first gear. The car was roaring. Gopalji's face became a little awkward.

After taking about seven turns he stopped the car on the side and switched on the park lights. Gopalji went out of the car and looked around. After a few moments he came back inside the car.

Grandpa raised his eyebrows looking at Gopalji.

'That is the way towards the Hospital' He said and pointed towards an unpaved road.

The road was fully covered with brown leaves. It was abandoned years ago.

'Are you sure?' grandpa asked, looking at the road.

'Yes, according to him it is the only way known' Gopalji said, being a little confused.

Grandpa looked again towards the road. The place was calm.

'Do we need to ask someone?' he said.

'Okay, I will search for someone here' Gopalji said and stepped out of the car.

Grandpa also came out of the car to find someone. They didn't find anyone around. Grandpa took his phone to check in Google maps. The network was down.

'Nobody sir' Gopalji said after returning to the car.

'The network is also down' grandpa said and looked at the lonely horrifying road.

'Can we proceed?' Gopalji asked for approval.

'Yes, it is the only way for us and we don't have much time to lose' grandpa said and got inside the car.

Gopalji drove the car slowly through the narrow unused road. The road was fully covered with brown leaves. The road was a little bumpy. Grandpa held on to the handle above his door.

They went ahead. They were alone on that road. Road led to a forest, huge trees and the noise of cicadas all around. Gopalji was completely concentrating on the bumpy road. Meanwhile, grandpa was looking around for a human being. Suddenly, a blasting sound came from the rear end of the car. Gopalji hit the brakes and looked towards the rear by putting his head outside through the window. He couldn't see anything.

Gopalji removed his seat belt, opened his door and got down. He moved towards the rear wheels. The tire was fully useless. Gopalji kicked the tire by his right leg and turned around and stood supporting the car.

Grandpa opened his door and went out to enquire.

'Is it gone?' grandpa asked.

'Yeah' Gopalji said in a plain voice.

'What can we do now? Do we have a spare tire?' grandpa asked.

'No sir, It is already punctured' Gopalji said and went and got inside the car.

Grandpa also went inside the car, Gopalji tried to call up the shopkeeper who navigated them to this road.

'You have his contact?' grandpa said.

Gopalji nodded his head in affirmation.

'Nice!' replied grandpa.

'But no network sir' Gopalji said.

'This place......' grandpa said in frustration and hit the dashboard. Gopalji looked at grandpa uncomfortably.

'Sorry, my bad' grandpa apologized.

A knock on the window of Gopalji.

Gopalji turned towards his closed window. An old man with white beard was looking inside.

The old man was wearing grey pyjamas and a black overcoat. He was holding a wooden stick and had a silver stud earring on his left ear. He looked like a hippy model that we see in Goan beaches.

He knocked again on the glass window. Gopalji was a little terrified but it was the only help they could get in the lonely forest.

Gopalji opened his door slowly. The old man moved back. Gopalji opened the door fully and got out.

'Why are you here?' the old man asked.

'We are on the way to Benjamin's psychological centre. Our tire is gone' Gopalji said, pointing to the flat rear tire.

'Who uses this road, this is a very dangerous road, and by God's grace you are still alive' the old man said.

'Do you know any mechanics here' Gopalji asked.

'No one will come here, let the car be here. I will direct you to the hospital' the old man said and started walking forward.

'Sir, come let's go' Gopalji told grandpa.

They both started to walk.

'Why are you here?' an old man asked while walking.

'To see a friend's daughter' Gopalji said.

Gopalji and the old man were walking together and grandpa was a little left behind them, walking slowly.

The way was in a dense forest. Monkeys were hanging from the trees looking at them. They kept on walking through the way following the old man.

They reached the shore of a broad river. The river was not full. They were able to walk through the rocks. Gopalji and the old man started crossing the river through rocky parts.

Gopalji reached the center of the river when he turned back to check on grandpa. He was having trouble crossing the river. Grandpa was in doubt whether he could move through the river.

Gopalji turned back towards grandpa by leaving the old man. Gopalji reached and gave a hand to grandpa. He extended his hands holding Gopalji's.

With the help of Gopalji grandpa took his first steps on the rocks.

'Thank you' grandpa said by stressing the word "you" when he pressed his left leg hard for the next step.

Gopalji turned towards the old man in front.

Gopalji stopped moving. And turned his head one eighty degrees.

'What happened?' grandpa asked when he stopped moving.

'Where is he?' Gopalji asked, looking around.

'Who are you talking about?' grandpa asked and looked in the direction where Gopalji was looking.

'He was there... an old man, who was giving us directions' Gopalji said to grandpa.

'Who? There was no one. You only said that you know the way' grandpa said looking at Gopalji's face.

'What? He said he knows the way, that's why we started

walking' Gopalji said.

'Nobody was there, you were walking alone' grandpa said.

'What I don't understand' Gopalji said.

'Is it a mind game, beware they are playing with our mind.' Grandpa said and moved forward.

They both reached the middle of the river. They saw a board on the opposite shore. They moved forwards and slowly reached the other shore.

Gopalji was still confused about the old man's incident. Grandpa went near the board.

'This board shows the way to the hospital' grandpa said.

'So they were leading us here, I really don't know the way' Gopalji said.

They both went silent. After a moment, Gopalji initiated a conversation.

'I think we need to find the villain and save Reghu' Gopalji said and walked towards the direction shown in the board without giving a chance for a reply.

Grandpa looked at the empty river for a few seconds.

'I'm tired' grandpa said and held Gopalji's shoulder with his skinny hands.

'I think we are close' He said and held grandpa's hands and pulled softly.

They walked and saw a large gate at a distance.

'Finally, we reached' Gopalji said, his face glowing.

'Really?' grandpa asked and looked towards the gate.

They reached near the closed gate.

A large old bungalow, in the middle of the forest. It was like a fort and had a huge garden in front. Some gardeners were setting the plants and some were watering the blossoming flowers. As they reached the gate a security came in front of the gate on the other side. He smiled and opened the gate. He called them towards his post.

'Sir, your name?' security asked grandpa politely.

'Raj Jadhav' grandpa said and looked back at the magnificent architecture.

'Nandha Gopal' Gopalji said.

'I know sir' Security said and closed the register.

They walked together towards the entrance of the bungalow. Some people were walking without any concern, thinking about something. They were wearing glowing white pyjamas and a T-shirt.

They went inside the bungalow and Gopalji went to the front desk. Grandpa took a seat on the couch, he was really tired from the long walk.

A cute girl came with a glass of water for grandpa. Grandpa took it without any hesitation and drank it.

'Hello sir, how can I help you?' the girl sitting in the front desk asked.

'We want to see Miss. Ashima' Gopalji said.

'Ok sir, the purpose of the visit?' she asked, holding a pen.

Grandpa finished his important drink and placed the glass on the small table in front of him. He took his phone out and looked for a signal. It was showing two bricks of a network.

He switched on the data and opened his lazy WhatsApp. The screen started jumping as he hadn't opened it for a couple of days.

After a few seconds, the screen stabilized. He saw a message from Amaana.

He opened it first to learn about Reghu.

"Grandpa, I tried to call you but couldn't reach you. That's why I messaged."

"Reghu is feeling good now and he wants to see you"

"We are coming back home tomorrow"

"Bye grandpa hope you are doing well"

Grandpa pressed the back button. Gopalji came to him and made himself comfortable on the couch.

'All set, we can see her in ten minutes' Gopalji said.

Grandpa raised his head from his mobile and looked at Gopalji.

'They are coming home tomorrow' grandpa said.

'Who?' Gopalji asked.

'Reghu and Amaana' grandpa said.

'Why so fast?' Gopalji got confused.

'Reghu wants to see me' grandpa said.

'Hmm, so we need to go back by evening' Gopalji said.

'It's already evening Gopal' grandpa said and continued.

'I already messaged back that we are out and will reach by tomorrow evening.'

While they were talking, the young receptionist came towards them.

'Sir, can we move?' she said politely.

Gopalji and grandpa stood up. Grandpa put his mobile phone in his left pocket.

Three of them walked through the long hallway.

'Sir, she has been a little violent for the past two days, so we don't appreciate close contact with her' the young lady said in her sweet voice.

Gopalji looked at grandpa with a frown on his face.

They were taken to a narrow path. The lights got dimmer. The way became lonely and silent. At the end there was a man standing with a lathi in his hand.

They reached the end of the narrow dim path. The guard didn't give any reaction.

'Prem, they are here to see her' she said and turned back to them.

'She has been a little violent for the last few days so that's why she is inside this, be careful' she said to Gopalji and grandpa and returned through the dim narrow path.

Grandpa went near the iron bars of the door and looked inside. The room was empty. Some Light was coming through a window on the west side. All corners were dark.

Gopalji asked the guard to open the door. But he refused without any reply.

'We know her and she knows us, our visit will help her' Gopalji tried to convince.

Guard opened the gate slowly with disapproval. Gopalji and grandpa went inside. After they entered, a guard locked the door from outside.

They looked around in the cell.

'Ashima, Ashima' Gopalji called out looking into dark corners.

Suddenly she came in front of the only window. Grandpa and Gopalji looked towards her but because of the light from behind they couldn't see her face. She was wearing a white skirt and her hair was open and it was covering her face. She was not looking at them. She moved slowly towards them. Grandpa took a step back as she moved towards him. He stopped moving when he touched Gopalji.

Grandpa looked at Gopalji and again looked towards the window. She disappeared.

Suddenly, 'Who are you?' she asked furiously at grandpa from his left. Grandpa turned to her. She was close. Grandpa moved back and held his hands on his chest.

'Ashima' Gopalji called.

She looked at him and became silent.

'I am Dhamodhar's father, Raj Jadhav' grandpa said.

'Reghu's grandfather' she said in an unclear voice.

'Yes, do you know him?' grandpa asked politely.

'He changed my whole life and family' she said and moved back to the dark corner.

CHAPTER SEVENTEEN

POV of Ashima

My twelfth result came. I passed with distinction. Everybody was in its thrill. Mom and dad were so happy, but I was confused about my next step.

I really didn't have a dream.

"Why a girl like me didn't have a dream?" I asked myself several times looking at the mirror.

"What do I have to become, a doctor, a professor or what?" I am confused.

"But I always admired about one person, Advocate uncle"

My father had a friend, who was an Advocate. He was a regular visitor at our house. His stories about the cases he appeared at always thrilled me. I'm so thrilled about that job. I wanted to be an Advocate.

"I'm an ordinary Indian girl, will my dad and mom allow me to choose Law" my thoughts made me restless.

"Where to start? when to start?, how to convince them?" my mind keeps on asking these questions.

I decided to discuss it at dinner. I prepared myself for the mission.

Mom had made Phirni (a Punjabi sweet) for dinner. I loved Phirni.

Mom, dad and my little brother were having dinner, I was waiting for a good time. But all were concentrating on the delicious dinner. I couldn't enjoy the dinner at all.

'I want to discuss something with all of you' I said.

All eyes focused on me with anticipation.

'I want to become a lawyer' I said without any break in between the sentence and looked down at my plate and started eating like a beast.

'What? Lawyer?' Mom asked.

"Oh, it's going be an action-thriller here" I thought.

'Is that a job for a girl?' mom asked.

Dad looked at her and winked his eyes. My mom became silent.

'It is a very difficult and tough career, you ask our uncle, he will tell you' dad said and put an end to the conversation.

"That's it?"

All dads have this ultimate power of ending a conversation so fast before it gets nasty.

Everyone went back to eating dinner.

After dinner, I went to my room and waited for everyone to go to sleep.

I took the landline phone and called my uncle. It was eleven at night. He picked up the phone anyway.

'Hello' he said, he sounded drowsy.

'It's me Ashima' I whispered.

'What happened beta?' he asked after clearing his voice.

'Nothing uncle, I want to become an advocate, I need your support here' I said politely.

'Oh that was the thing. Tomorrow I'm coming there to congratulate you. The results are really great' He said and hung up.

The morning rays came inside my room. I woke up and went to the kitchen. I started pretending like a good girl, because I wanted their permission to pursue law.

By morning eleven, Advocate uncle came home with a rectangular gift box.

'Congratulations beta' he said and gave me the gift. It was heavy.

After a few minutes, dad put the subject in. My heart started beating faster.

'If she likes that profession then she could shine in that, women have a main role in law and their importance is getting higher every day.' Uncle said.

'Dealing with criminals will not be good for a woman' my mom scored from the side.

'Advocate means not only dealing with criminals. Ladies are experts in Divorce cases, she can either be a separator or a joiner, and it's up to you' Uncle said.

I felt a little relaxed. All oppositions went weak, uncle continued.

'Satisfaction in what we are doing is important, even if it is robbery. Then only there will be a content life' uncle said and concluded.

'So which college is best for her?' Dad asked.

All set. My Advocate uncle saved me.

'Symbiosis Law school, Pune' Uncle said.

"So Symbiosis Pune" I thought with excitement.

'Make that gift your life' uncle said pointing to the gift box as he was about to leave.

I opened the gift wrapper. It was a book. I unwrapped it. It was written "The Indian Penal Code from K.D. Gaur". The book had a hard cover. The cover photo was of a hammer used by judges. I had seen that hammer once when I went with my dad to meet the advocate uncle at the court.

I opened the heavy book, the fragrance of newness spread all around inside my room. I took a random page out of curiosity.

"Section 420."

I went to the notice board to check my assigned hostel room. Just as in the movies, a large crowd was already in front of the notice board. But I had to find my room because dad was waiting outside in the car with my luggage. I went closer to the notice board. It was too crowded. I moved through the gaps and reached at a position that enabled me to read the miniature text.

'Ashima.....' I whispered and looked closely at the list.

'Are you Ashima?' a tall girl with deep red lipstick asked.

'Yes, do you know me?' I asked.

'One two seven' she said and moved out of the crowd.

'What?'

'Come on, let's go. I'm your roommate' she said.

'Oh really?' I said and went out of the crowd.

'Hey wait, I think I lost something in the crowd.' I said.

'May be your virginity' she said and laughed.

'If you go back again you will lose yourself. But I really enjoyed it.' She said and giggled.

We left the college.

'What's your name?' I asked.

'Rashi.... Rashi Mandanna' she said while walking.

'From south?' I asked deliberately.

This question is always asked to every Indian, South, North, East, West, and Middle. Some people go for a little more specific, north – East, South – West, etc.

'Yeah, my parents hail from Karnataka. But I was born and brought up in Mumbai.' She said it was by heart.

I went to our room with my dad. Rashi opened the white single door of room One two seven on the first floor. The room was so cute and had a decent space to accommodate ourselves for four years. Rashi took the bed near to the window and I took the bed near to the study table. The room was well maintained and tidy.

Dad unloaded all my stuff. He was silent that day. His face was gloomy. At the time of leaving he took my hand and placed a card in my palm and left.

It was nothing else, a debit card linked with dad's phone.

My first day at college. I and Rashi walked slowly towards our block. I was a little afraid, the stories about ragging that my cousin sister told me were really terrible.

The college was built in an Arabic style. The walls were covered with tiles and it was uniformly maintained everywhere. A well maintained architecture. I got a scholarship to learn, so I didn't have to pay any fees. For a girl like me, Symbiosis Law College is just like a dream, but the scholarship program made my dream come true.

I was carrying a bag. I was wearing a black salwar kameez and my hair was tied simply, in a pony tail. I kept myself under cover. Rashi had a great makeover and her lips were even redder than yesterday.

I crossed the gate and walked without glancing at the seniors. I was humming inside.

"Please God save me from ragging"

'Hey' a voice came from my left. I didn't stop. I continue to march. Rashi also accompanied me.

'Hey, you in black. Stop right there' the voice came again.

This time I couldn't ignore it. I stopped at the moment and took a deep breath. I turned slowly towards the direction of the sound. I didn't raise my head, I was looking at the ground.

'Hello, is there any problem? Can you please look at my

face?' a male voice came.

He gestured to Rashi to move on.

I was really nervous. All the horrible stories that my cousin said were echoing in my ears.

I looked up.

A senior was standing in front of me; two girls were sitting on the ramp of the stairs. A handsome man was sitting behind them and he was not looking at me. He was wearing a jacket. His hair was shiny and it was smooth.

'What's your name?' one of the girls asked.

'Ashima' I said. My hands were shivering.

The guy at the back turned and looked at me. His eyes were glittering. He had a sexy black beard, which was perfectly trimmed.

He looked at me and paused for a second.

'Leave' he said in his firm, manly voice.

All the others looked at him and without any hesitation they obeyed him.

'Ok Ashima, nice to meet you, bye' the other person said.

I turned to my left and walked straight inside the campus.

'What happened? What did he ask?' Rashi asked curiously.

'Nothing, the other guy asked me to leave after hearing my name' I said.

'It's Reghu' she said, her voice filled with great emotion.

'You know him?' I asked.

'Not really, but he is this rich guy from Mumbai'

I looked at him again from a distance, turned and went to my class.

Our class was on the second floor. We took the stairs and went to a corner. Our class was the last on that floor. We entered the class, all were sitting quietly as they were all strangers. An equally divided class in the category of gender.

Rashi took the charge and went in front to a right corner at the sixth row. That place was basically the last. I couldn't stop her so I followed her. Our class was tiered. I haven't seen that kind of class room in reality.

The bell rang sharply. It was an automatic bell. Our faculty came inside with a book in her hand. It was large and kept it on the table provided for the faculty.

She was a middle aged woman with glasses fixed at the tip of her nose. She was wearing a saree which was formal, not decorated as Rashi's glittering top.

All stood up and smiled at her. I was expecting a long "Good morning Miss" but that didn't happen.

She told me to sit with a hand gesture.

She took the heavy book from the table and held it forward. 'Indian penal code' we all read.

'This is your Bible or Bhagavad Gita or Quran' she said.

Everyone focused deeply on the book. I was not surprised as I have already heard that dialogue from my uncle. After showing the heavy book, she opened it and read loudly and firmly.

"I do solemnly, sincerely and truly declare and affirm that the evidence I shall give shall be the true the whole truth and nothing but the truth."

The intro was mass, she nailed it. But the days of monotonous hours were about to come.

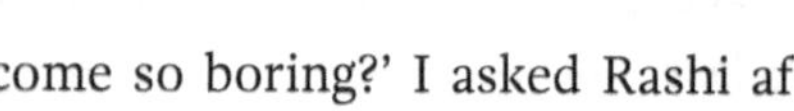

'How did this law become so boring?' I asked Rashi after hearing the long boring classes.

We were sitting on the loan after a boring session. She was very busy with picking her daily collection of boys. She likes muscular boys if they are rich, a typical Indian girl. Sometimes I feel like she used to come here only for that, but still a virgin and single. "How is she still a virgin?"

'Hey Reghu coming' She said after ignoring my statement.

I looked at him, he was much more handsome today. Rashi was enjoying looking at him.

'Stop yaar, he will get pregnant' I said and moved her head in a different direction.

Her face rebounded on him again. I understood she won't budge.

'Rashi, go and tell him if you like him' I said.

'No way, I will make him come behind me' she said with pride.

'Really?' I asked with confusion.

She turned her face slowly towards me. "Will she beat me for that?" Her face was really horrifying.

My face changed as I saw her.

Her face slowly changed into a smile again.

'Afraid?' she asked, laughing.

"Why did she do that? I'm too small compared to her fist. I need to be careful" I thought.

'Let's go?' she asked.

I looked at my watch.

'Yeah, it's time'.

We went together to our class at the corner. And again to another corner in the class. "I'm totally cornered". Another faculty came. A young gentleman. He was a real lawyer before. So he had a lot of experience, his classes were full of examples and his classes were far better than the other dry classes.

He always wore a suit in class. It was well fit and it made him very handsome. He used to take criminal law for us, hence it was interesting.

As usual he started with one of his cases of kidnapping. The stories were very thrilling and it was always like those John

Abraham movies. Sometimes Rashi would say that these stories were copied from Hollywood movies. But I didn't want to believe it, because I wanted this class to remain interesting.

Everyone was listening attentively to his adventurous case studies, and suddenly a group of seniors entered our class.

'What happened?' Faculty asked the group.

'Nothing sir, just a minute' the one in front of the procession said.

'You guys spoiled my thrilling case' he said.

'Identity case or the Orphan case' a voice came from inside the group.

A silly laugh spread inside the class. But I didn't understand the humour. I looked at Rashi with my eyebrows up in question.

'Those are famous crime thrillers in Hollywood' she said.

I giggled but the whole class was silent. Everybody heard my giggle. Sir turned furiously towards me.

"Oh shit, I'm done." I thought, my heart started beating fast.

'Sir, so let me speak' suddenly Reghu came in front from inside and cleverly changed the topic.

"I'm safe" I let out an audible sigh of relief.

'Hello everyone, the day after tomorrow we are conducting the fresher's party for all of you from evening six. Hope all of you will join us and let's make this a chance to get to know each other well and have some fun' Reghu said and turned back.

Whole group went out of the class, and the professor continued his Hollywood stories again. I listened to all the thrilling stories attentively as I didn't watch much Hollywood movies.

'What should I wear? I don't have anything good' I said looking at my small wardrobe.

'No party wear?' Rashi asked.

She was straightening her hair facing the small mirror on the wall.

'Hey, wait I have one' she said after thinking.

'Your dress... It would be like a gown of ghosts for me' I said.

'I had ordered it online, it came too small, even Sunny Leona will be shy to wear it' she said and laughed.

Rashi will not forget to laugh at her own jokes. She really enjoyed her jokes.

'Did you order a thread?' This time I laughed at my joke, but she didn't.

She gave me a pathetic glance. I understood the level of my joke from her face.

After straightening she opened her trolley and took out a royal blue party wear. And she took a packet too.

'Try it' she said and gave me the dress.

I changed my clothes and put on her party wear.

It was small, it reached only till my knees, and I really felt uncomfortable.

"If mom sees me in this dress, I will be out of the whole of Punjab" I thought after looking at me.

'Wow, perfect. You really look like a princess' Rashi said and came near me and held my shoulders with a broad smile.

'Really?'

'I will not allow you to go like this. You will be a huge competition for me' she said with a naughty smile.

"I know," I thought.

'One more small task' she said and bent down.

I thought she was going to look from beneath, by my

reflection I kept my hands like Marilyn Monroe.

'I'm taking your sandals off' she said looking up.

She moved her hands quickly and pulled my androgenic hair.

'Awe' I cried. My eyes filled.

'What in hell with you?' I asked furiously.

She took that packet in her hands.

'Let's wax you.'

'No way' I said and started running inside the room.

As she had long arms, she just stood up and caught me.

'No, no, no' I cried.

'Yes, yes, yes' she said and threw me onto the bed.

She opened the pack by biting it and took one weapon out, she laughed like a witch and came near me.

'Please, please, please' I plead.

She pasted it on my right leg. I looked at it.

And she started rubbing it vigorously due to which it became warmer and I could feel the warmth on my skin through it.

'One two' she pulled the sheet out.

"I was expecting three and four"

Everything came out.

A horrible experience, my legs were glittering in red.

She went on pasting it on other legs and made my soul fly each time.

'Done, how are your legs now?' Rashi said.

'It's still burning' I said when we walked towards the loan for the fresher's party. The sun became dull, the sky was orange.

We walked slowly through the pathway. The party had already begun. Some games were going on. We joined the rest of our classmates on the right side of the stage.

Reghu was the coordinator of the stage. He was really busy, the two girls I saw with him on the first day were with him as his personal assistants. He was wearing a black jacket and blue jeans. His watch reflected the lights that came from the stage to my eyes.

After the games they had arranged a DJ. Everyone went crazy with the DJ. I also joined my classmates, but I was really horrible at dancing. Rashi was in a great mood. Her red lips were really highlighted in the dark.

"How is it glowing so much?" I thought.

I got really tired after one hour and I went to get some air. I went a little far from the crowd and sat down on a chair. I could see Rashi doing freaky steps. I smiled at her when she looked at me while doing them.

Some boys were approaching near my chair, but I didn't mind them. They came near me and circled around me.

'Hello, got tired?' One among them asked.

As it was dark I couldn't see their faces.

'No, just taking a break' I said.

'Do you want company?'

'No, I'm good'

'Why do you don't want our company?' his tone changed.

I stood up to leave.

'Hey where are you going?' he asked by holding my hand tight.

I pulled my hand back. Their faces were still not visible to me. My heart started beating fast. Even if I scream no one will hear me because of the loud music.

'Hey look at her skirt, its very small' he said and moved his hand down slowly under my skirt. All other laughed and encouraged him. My skirt raised as his hand went in. I thought of running away.

One guy from the back held my right hand. I really started to breathe fast. My eyes started to blur. My pressure rose as my skirt was raised.

'Hey, what's happening here?' A strong voice came from my left side.

Rapidly, my hands were released. The hand that went on to touch my V slipped away. I took a deep breath. My eyes cleared. They looked at the bold voice in the dark.

They moved rapidly away in different directions. I went down on the bench. I got totally exhausted. I haven't felt like this before in my life.

I understood my father's protection, when I was with him.

The saviour came to me and he knelt down and raised my head with his tender soft hands.

'Are you okay?' he asked.

Really my relay was gone. I couldn't concentrate on what he was asking.

Slowly I came back to normal. He kept his silence for a moment as I was not giving him any answers to his questions.

'Are you okay?' he repeated, this time he was more sweet.

'Yeah, what was that? I really got...' I said.

'No, nothing. Everything is just fine. Don't think about it.' He said.

I looked into his eyes. His eyes were pure and were glowing with care. It was Reghu. He smiled as I looked at his face.

Rashi came near us as a hulk with some of our classmates.

'What happened?' she asked in a hurry.

'Nothing happened, she will tell you later' he said looking at her.

'Is she alright?' concerned Rashi.

'Yeah, better now. Right Ashima?' he said.

"He remembered my name, how?" even in that situation I

was thinking about this. "Yeah, I'm a girl."

He moved back and Rashi came near me and sat down on the bench. Slowly I got back to normal. I stood up and moved with Rashi back to the group.

I wanted to see him to thank him for saving me. But I couldn't find him in the crowd. I waited for the program to end.

CHAPTER EIGHTEEN

POV of Ashima

"There he is, if I go will it be wrong? No, I want to thank him" I made up my mind.

I walked slowly towards him, he was busy settling the music freaks. He felt my presence and turned towards me.

'Are you okay now?' Reghu asked me politely.

'What happened sister? You didn't like my music?' DJ asked me.

'Enough bro, leave, all good. I will deal with this' Reghu said to him.

Reghu came near me.

'Are you okay?' he asked again.

'Yeah, I'm alright. Let's have a walk?' I asked.

'Yeah sure'

'Thank you Reghu' I said after taking a few steps.

'Thank you for what. It's my responsibility' he said with a pleasing smile.

We walked through the pathway, at the end there was a light. It made the whole pathway clear.

'You are Ashima right?'

'Yeah, we met on the first day' I said.

'Yeah, you are from Punjab' he asked with curiosity.

'Yes, but my family is settled in Pune. My father works here in the ammunition factory.' I said.

'Oh that's cool' he said and shot me with his hand gun.

I acted like I'm falling and we giggled.

'I'm from Maharashtra' Reghu said.

'I know'

'How?' he asked.

'My roommate is also from Maharashtra, she told me about you' I said quickly.

'Ok...ok, who is she?'

'Rashi, the girl who came to me after that incident. Tall, red lipstick' I said by showing hand gestures.

'Yeah, you don't like red lipstick.' he asked.

"How does he know that? These men find everything" I thought.

'Yeah' I said.

We walked a lot from the party plot. The place was lonely and was in deep silence. I felt a little cold as my dress was short and translucent. I folded my hands.

Reghu took his jacket off and covered me. Most of the movies I have seen have the same scene, and now I also went through that scene.

"Why do boys do this? Is that to show they care about us? But did Reghu really care about me" I smiled inside and looked at him. His eyes were glittering in the light coming from the end.

He looked at me and he put his masterpiece smile on his face.

"Oh so cute, I want to pinch his cheeks, so cute" I thought.

'Can I ask you something?' Reghu asked.

I nodded.

'If you are free. Can we go out for dinner this weekend?' He asked politely.

"How can a girl say NO to a handsome loving man for a date, is that a date? Wow my first date" my heart started jumping but I didn't show anything.

'Yeah ok, this Saturday? Is it Okay?' I said.

'Yeah perfect' he said.

We turned around and started walking back. Rashi was looking from a distance, I could see her smile on her face.

'Your family?' Reghu asked to avoid silence.

'Dad, mom and a little brother'

'And you?'

'Dad and grandpa' Reghu said.

'Mom?'

'She died ten years back' Reghu said in a plain voice'

'I'm sorry'

'It's alright, old stories' he said.

Suddenly I stepped on a small pebble on the pathway and I moved slightly towards Reghu and our hands stroked softly. Butterflies started to fly in my tummy, when my skin touched his hairy smooth skin.

I smiled but Reghu didn't respond or maybe I didn't see anything.

We reached back near Rashi.

'Hi Rashi' Reghu greeted.

She was surprised.

'Hi Reghu, I'm from Maharashtra' Rashi said.

'I know, your bestie told me everything about you' Reghu said and looked at me. I smiled back.

'Ok, Ashy. Bye, see you' Reghu said.

'Bye' I said.

'What, Ashy? New nickname' Rashi asked and came near me, hugged me with a smile.

"Ashy, nice I like it."

'Rashi I want to go shopping, I don't have a good one to wear for the date' I said.

'Yeah, let's go' Rashi said.

We went for shopping at the nearest Mall. The day was hot, so we took an auto to the mall.

The air condition inside the mall made us back to normal from the temperature outside. Rashi knew a designer shop there and she was looking for it. Finally we found our destination Zepeda Fashion.

The store was amazing and was full of colours. The dim yellow light inside the shop made all dyed clothes more vivid.

'Last time it was dark, let's go for some light shades' Rashi said as a professional costume designer.

As I was pretty bad in dressing and shopping, I gave all my costume administration to her.

She went through a lot of designs and finally brought some selected pieces to me. All were light shades. My eyes stuck at a glowing grey fit and flare frock. The frock was glittering in the yellow light.

Rashi directed me towards a trial room. I went inside and took off my clothes and then wore a new dress. I found myself so elegant in the mirror.

I came out with a smile. Rashi looked at me with her eyebrows up and gave the approval for the Fit and Flare.

'Shopping is not yet over, we need to buy silver metallic heels, the same metallic clutch and a non- wired inner.' She said.

My eyes went to the price tag. And my heart broke.

'Am I going for a ramp walk?' I said as I saw the price tag.

'These are all on me' Rashi said and gave her debit card.

'I will pay you later' I said. But Rashi didn't respond to it.

We went to other shops and bought the special requirements as recommended by Rashi.

By evening she found out the perfect combo for me for the

special date with the special man.

"Today I am going for my first date, with the super cool Reghu. Wow" I woke up with great happiness. My face was glowing like the sun. I didn't know why I was smiling all the time without any reason.

'Hey, today is your date' Rashi said with enormous happiness.

'Yeah, I know' I said.

'So we need to wax' Rashi said.

"She really enjoys waxing me. God please give me a chance to wax her too" I thought.

Today's waxing was comparatively less painful. After that was done I changed my clothes.

The time had come. I got ready with the new metallic clutch and heels.

'Wow, you are a princess now' Rashi said and took a selfie with me.

'Where is the dinner?' Rashi asked enthusiastically.

'Alto Vino' I said.

'Italian, signora' Rashi said in a wild Italian accent.

I went out and took an auto to Alto Vino. The sun was about to disappear. The sky was already dim. A nice romantic soft breeze was flowing all over. I am still smiling without any reason. Sometimes the auto driver was concerned about my smile.

I reached Alto Vito, I took out my phone and there was a message from Reghu.

'I'm here, waiting for you'

Alto vino is a modern Italian hotel, it was decorated with crystals. The beautiful crystals glittered when the lights fell on them.

I entered through the front door. Reghu was sitting straight facing the door. His eyes showed excitement. Maybe because of me.

I walked slowly towards him in an attitude with my metallic accessories. As I reached near our special couple table, Reghu stood up and pulled the chair for me gently. I smiled and took my seat.

The table was empty except, two stemware for wine. Reghu took his seat and at the same time a good looking server came with a bottle of red wine and poured it in my glass, then in Reghu's.

'You look so beautiful' Reghu said and took the crystal glass in his right hand.

I took my glass in my right hand.

'To my beautiful Ashy' Reghu said and toasted.

I smiled. We tossed our glasses. I took a small sip of the red wine. It was a really balanced pure wine.

We didn't order anything, everything was already set. One after the other it happened. We talked a lot about each other, we laughed a lot, and time went by so fast.

We got our molten lava cake and butterscotch ice cream. The food was very tasty but the conversation was tastier. Our first date was about to die at Alto Vito.

'I will drop you, it's late' Reghu said.

He took his black Polo and came in front of the restaurant. I got inside his car.

The car had a special fragrance. Reghu turned on the music, my favourite song came on.

"Pee loon" Emirian Hisami and Preachy.

He was well prepared for our date.

We took our way home. The fragrance and the beautiful romantic songs made me high, but I kept myself under control.

Reghu stopped his Polo on a lonely street, my heart started beating faster. He switched on the small light inside the car and looked at me. My face went blank.

'This is my home, I'm living here.' Reghu said and showed a bungalow through the right window.

A beautiful bungalow, only a light was on in front of the house. As it was dark I couldn't see much. The house was huge. And had large pillars.

'If you don't mind, let's have a coffee' He requested.

"No, Ashima. Go to your hostel. It's already late. Don't go inside. It would be hard for you to resist." My mind started talking like my mom.

'Please?' Reghu asked with a polite but firm voice.

All gone. I nodded.

We stepped out of the car and walked towards the house. The street was calm and lonely.

'Are you living here alone?' I asked.

'Yes' he replied and took the keys from his pocket. He opened the double-door entrance and got inside and welcomed me.

The lights were already on inside. A pleasant music started inside the house. The guest room was magnificent. All the furniture looked like an antique model, which were like British homes in Lagaan.

"Reghu loves antiques. Am I an antique?" I thought.

'Have a tour meanwhile, I will prepare some coffee for you' Reghu said and left me alone in the large guest room.

I went to some rooms. All rooms are very clean and very well organised. All the rooms had paintings and heavy curtains.

I went near a huge glass, I could see the street through the glass. Still the street was calm. I listened to the music and kept my eyes on the lonely street.

Reghu came near me and hugged me from behind with a cup of hot coffee. His arms wrapped around me and his head was on my right shoulder. I didn't resist, I enjoyed his warmth. I took the coffee from him, but he didn't move. We stood together near the glass for a few minutes.

I finished my coffee and turned around. Our eyes met. I could feel his heavy breath. My eyes closed and I moved closer to him.

'Let's have some steps?' Reghu said.

I opened my eyes. Reghu increased the volume of the music a bit. He held out his left hand for me to hold. I held his left hand with mine and moved closer to him. He held my navel with his right hand, and I moved my hand to his shoulders. We moved slowly with the romantic beats. He moved softly, and I moved with his steps. I started to immerse myself in the steps.

Reghu moved his right leg between my legs. We came closer again. This time I can't lose him. Our eyes again locked and our moves became sedated.

Reghu came closer to me. Our foreheads touched, our noses met, lastly our lips. We connected.

That kiss lasted for a long time. His tender lips were cold. We went so deep. We closed our eyes. My hands moved up and reached his hair.

Our days of love began with the steps we moved together to the romantic beats.

I became a regular visitor to his bungalow. Even a lot of my stuff was in his room. We practically started living together. My life turned a whole 180°. My mind had already started planning about my future with him and our children.

Reghu was waiting for me under our so-called "Groot".
Groot was a giant tree where Reghu saved me that time
from those freaks. It became our hangout place in college.
We called him "Groot".
Reghu was looking more handsome every day, maybe my
eyes were now under my heart's control.
I went behind him and hugged him from behind tightly. He
always knew that it would be me, he turned his head with a
smile and gave a kiss on my cheeks.
'My lady, why late?' he asked with a cute silly smile.
I went to his right and sat down with him, held his average
muscular right hand and laid my head on his arm.
'What happened? Romantic approach?' he asked.
'I'm always romantic, that's why' I said in a naughty tone.
'Tell me. What's your plan for the weekend?' he asked.
'Let's go for a long ride, on my bike'
'On a bike? Where?'
I nodded.
'Okay, let's go. I have a place to show you' he said in
excitement.
'Where?' I was amused.
'Surprise princess, wait for it' he said.
'Hey lovebirds' Johnson asked and interrupted us. Johnson
was his close friend.
'Yeah man?' Reghu asked.
'Hey Ashima, I'm taking your Reghu for a minute. Can I?'
He asked me.
I nodded with a blank smile.

I heard the horn from outside. I was in my hostel room getting ready for the long ride with Reghu. I was wearing a casual dress for the trip. I carried a handbag with me.

I came out of my room and looked for him. Reghu was waiting for me in a black Royal Enfield Classic 350. He was looking so powerful on the Classic. He was wearing a casual jacket and blue jeans. He knows exactly what to wear for each occasion. I love his dressing sense. He also liked mine, but my dresses were decided by Rashi.

I went down after giving a bye to my roommate Rashi, who was still under her blanket. I held on Reghu's shoulder and got on the bike. I was so excited about the trip.

'Comfortable?' he asked by looking back.

'No' I said and hugged him tightly from behind. 'Now comfortable'

He smiled and kick started the bike.

We moved through the lonely roads of Pune. The light cool breeze on my open hair. The cold breeze and the warmth from Reghu gave me eternal happiness. "To be with our loved ones is always a great feeling."

The whole city went behind us. Buildings and houses disappeared, full of green trees and the roads became zig-zag with curves. Riding on the Classic was so thrilling and made me very close to him for a long time. I placed my ears on him while he was talking. His body's vibrations were also so romantic.

After one hour of journey, we reached Panchgani. The best hill station near Pune.

Reghu pulled up at the roadside. He took his helmet off and looked at me by tilting his neck.

'Get down, we need to walk' Reghu said.

I came down from the bike. Reghu held my hands and pulled me across the road.

We passed through a gap between two huge trees. The whole place was a bit shady. I followed him through the green charming path.

After a long walk, Reghu went behind me. I looked at his weird action in confusion. He closed my eyes from behind with his palms and pushed me forward gently. He stopped me and took his hands from my eyes.

A small waterfall on the ledge. The clear water flowed freely from the highest and splashed on the rock.

I could see the whole road which we rode today, from the ledge. The sweet relaxing burbling of the waterfall, made that place even more special.

I turned around and hugged my man. I moved my head inside his jacket on his soft chest. Reghu held me with his hands.

We went near the waterfall. The droplets drizzled on my face. Cold and pure. I sprinkled some water on Reghu's face.

His face changed and he hugged me tightly, we went into the waterfall. The chilled water tumbled on us. I held him tighter. We stayed under it together.

We looked at each other. Our eyes exchanged our love. We slowly went down to sit on a rock under the waterfall. The chilled water was still falling on both of us. We didn't feel that cold as our bodies were sharing warmth.

Reghu moved his fingers from my forehead and progressed on the path of water. His hands moved slowly touching my lips and continued to conquer more of my body. His fingers were giving me a special sensation in my heart. His fingers passed my neck and reached my cleavage.

I took his hands with a naughty expression on my face and kept it on my head.

'Promise me, you won't leave me until I die' I said calmly.

Reghu smiled, and placed his palm on my head.

'I won't leave you'

'If you leave me, I will file a case on Section 420' I said and giggled.

We kissed with the pure chilling water from the hills. Our bodies and souls became one.

My life was going so good with Reghu. But God would not have allowed us to be happy always. We had a family issue. Maybe not that big an issue for me but it was for my parents. Even in that happiness, I felt blank.

I was sitting under the Groot, my face was not charming. Reghu sat down near me at the break. He looked at me.

'What happened? Are you upset?' Reghu asked with concern.

'Family matters' I said.

'If you don't mind, you can share it with me' Reghu said.

'My brother......' I said and paused.

'What happened to my jeeja?' Reghu asked.

"How can I say it now?" I was totally confused. "He is my man, I will tell him, he also had all the right to know about his wife's family" I thought and took the courage to tell him.

'My brother is a transgender, he wants to live like a girl' I said.

'What?' Reghu got surprised.

'Yeah, he can't live like a man' I said, confirming.

'Oh, that would create a big problem in your house' he said.

'Yes, dad and mom are very sad about it, and they are trying to bring him back' I said.

'How? Is it possible to change a person's soul? You need to support him'

'They sent him to a swami ji to change his mind' I said.

'What? They will definitely hurt him, he will not survive that, go and help him. Convince your mom and dad' Reghu said, holding my hands.

My eyes got wet. Slowly started to flow. Reghu held me on my shoulders.

'You should go and protect him. I will arrange everything for you to reach your house' Reghu said.

My brother came back from the ashram, he was badly injured. Still my dad was furious about his change. Dad doesn't care about his feelings. I tried to talk to him, but I couldn't do it. The whole situation was too bad.

My brother had a childhood friend, he came inside our house to visit him. My brother never spoke anything after returning from the ashram.

'Didi, where is he?' my friend asked.

'He is in the bedroom, he hasn't spoken a word till now' I said in pain.

He went inside the room slowly and towards my brother who was looking at the light coming from the small window in the morning.

They were talking about something, I didn't want to go near to distract them. Maybe my presence may stop their conversation.

I moved away from my bedroom. I really didn't know about the matter.

Suddenly dad came inside, and walked furiously towards the bedroom. He went there and started shouting at them. I got really scared because of my dad's odd actions. I have never seen him like this before.

Dad made my brother's friend get out of the house and was yelling harshly not to come back again.

"What did he do in this?" I thought about it and went to my brother. He was weeping inside. I went near him and sat next to him.

'Don't worry, I'm with you' I said.

Suddenly I heard my dad crying loudly. It was not of depression or sadness but a roar of pain.

I ran out of the bedroom to check what had happened. I locked the room from outside.

I came to the living room. Dad was lying on the floor. His head was bleeding and he was not moving.

Johnson stood in front of me with a metal rod in his right hand. I got really scared. I went near dad to wake him up. I couldn't speak anything. I looked at Johnson "Why?" in desperation.

I tried to wake my dad up. My mother came to the living room and saw my dad lying down.

'Who are you?' mom asked loudly and charged towards Johnson.

He blew the metal rod again hard again. She fell down. The blow was hard. There was no mercy.

My eyes started flowing unstoppably. My whole body started shivering. My mind collapsed. I couldn't control the shock watching my mom and dad on the floor wet in blood.

"He will kill me" I thought.

Suddenly Reghu came inside from behind and pushed him aside. Reghu rushed near me.

I was raised back on my foot by holding on my shoulders, I looked up. "He will kill me" I thought.

Reghu pulled me up and made me stand on my legs. Snapped his fingers in front of my eyes in an act to get back my focus.

'Sorry, I want to keep my promise. I won't leave you until you die' Reghu said.

"What is happening here? What is he talking about?" I couldn't think of anything.

'If I cheat you, you will file a case against me, right?' he asked and held me by my hair tightly and pulled it backwards.

'File it then, you bastard' he shouted loudly.

I couldn't speak. He raised the metal rod high to hit me on my head. My eyes started to flow but I didn't plead to him. Johnson Held the rod. Reghu looked back.

'We will definitely kill her, before that can I have her a bit, I always desired her' Johnson said.

Reghu released my hair and left the room. I went down as he released my hair. Johnson held my hands. I couldn't do anything. I was weak and trembling.

He pulled me and moved away from my dad and mom. He pulled me inside a room and closed the door. He removed his shirt aggressively and came near me.

I was already half dead. He hit me hard on my face. I turned and fell down. I tried to turn back up, but he pushed me back on my neck with his strong left hand. My throat was pressed on the floor. I couldn't even make a sound. I couldn't really breathe.

He ripped my skirt off. He tried to pull my top off. But I couldn't take it off. He pressed again on my neck. I opened my mouth to breathe, the force was intense. My eyes were burning and filled with tears of pain. He pulled up my top again. I became fully naked. I tried to reach him with my hands to push him away.

He took a flower pot from the table near us and hit me hard on my head. I cried in pain. My eyes started blurring.

My mind was unstable, I felt like my soul came out. I blacked out.

My whole body was in pain. I couldn't move my legs, they were totally paralysed. I opened my eyes.

'Finish her too' Johnson said to a goon.

'Boy, you go home with Reghu. I will handle this.' Reghu's father ordered Johnson.

Johnson left the room.

Reghu's father gestured to the goon to finish me.

He took a knife out and raised it against my naked body to stab me on my belly.

Suddenly a voice came from outside.

'Please don't kill her. Please leave her alone. I will do whatever you want. Please don't kill her' cried our advocate uncle.

Dhamodhar looked at him and raised his hands to stop the goon.

The Goon released me. I fell on the floor. He kicked on my face with his hard boot.

'Please don't do anything to her' uncle pleaded. He was holding my brother.

'Do you want to save both?' Dhamodhar asked harshly.

'Please, sir' he cried for my life.

I was already dead.

'Okay, I will leave her. But this boy needs to take all the responsibility of these two bodies.' Dhamodhar made an easy deal with him.

'Sir, please' he cried.

'Take her' Dhamodhar said furiously to goon.

The goon came again near me and pulled my hair up. I felt like my head was broken into two parts. I closed my eyes with pain, but I was not able to make any noise, my eyes were dry. He held his knife on my windpipe and pressed it against my skin. Blood came out.

'Okay sir, he will admit it' Uncle cried out loudly. He released my hair. Once again I came back to life from the edge of complete death. My face hit the floor. My hands were not strong enough to hold my body. My mind was not stable enough to take a reflex action. My body and mind were already damaged.

CHAPTER NINETEEN

POV of Third person

Grandpa couldn't look at her. He felt guilty. His eyes were wet after hearing about her life.

'I don't know how my children became like this?' Grandpa wept in pain.

'Now get out and try to save the rest of your family' she said with rage.

Grandpa stood up with pain, heart broken. He walked out of the cell in grief. Grandpa looked back into the cell with hands folded as an apology. But she already went back into dark shadows inside the cell.

Grandpa walked slowly through the narrow corridor in agony. He always tried to be a role model for his children and he was so proud to be a successful father, but now he found himself with nothing.

Gopalji walked with grandpa through the corridor without a word. Gopalji was in search of the killer but grandpa had already found the answer. Gopalji kept an eye on grandpa and moved behind him in disappointment.

'Sir, he will be the killer, her brother' Gopalji said.

'No, my children' grandpa sobbed in the lobby.

'But sir, we need to save Reghu' Gopalji tried to convince grandpa. But grandpa was completely blank and had lost all hope. Gopalji made him sit on the couch.

Gopalji went to the young lady at the reception.

'Ma'am is there any local guardian for Ashima' Gopalji asked politely.

'Let me check, please wait sir' she replied.

He went near grandpa and tried to console him.

'Sir, I have a contact number' the young lady said.

Gopalji put his hands in the pocket to take his mobile out. Grandpa raised his head when he heard about the contact number.

Gopalji did not have his phone. He searched all his pockets.

'Sir I think I kept my phone in the car.' Gopalji said as he couldn't find his phone.

'I have mine' grandpa said, his voice was terrible and took his phone out of his left pocket.

'Tell me beta' Grandpa said in grief.

'Sir it's, eight one two'

'Eight one two' Grandpa pressed the numbers slowly on the screen.

'Double nine' she said.

'Then?' Gopalji asked after grandpa was done dialling.

'Seven one seven four three' she completed.

'Seven one seven' Grandpa paused.

'Four three'

'Thank you beta' Grandpa said and pressed the green button in the bottom.

The screen changed to dialling.

The name came up "Amaana" appeared on the screen.

Grandpa gulped when he saw the name on the screen. His eyes wide open.

'Gopalji' grandpa screamed.

Gopalji, shocked by his scream, went near grandpa and held his hands. He looked at the screen. His face changed to red.

They took a Toyota Innova taxi from the hospital and returned to Mumbai.

Grandpa didn't even blink his eyes when they returned. Grandpa was afraid of calling her. He kept his phone in silent mode.

'Go fast' Gopalji kept instructing the driver.

Grandpa's face became pale. That trip back to Mumbai was very fast. They didn't waste even a minute.

Their car entered the porch and stopped. Grandpa got out of the car quickly. He went towards the entrance. He pushed the door open.

It was already open.

'Reghu……Reghu' grandpa screamed.

His voice started to tremble. He checked all the rooms, but couldn't find him.

'Sir' Gopalji called out loudly from outside.

Grandpa turned around and went back to the entrance.

'Sir' Gopalji said in frailty and pointed his right arm towards the small pool.

Grandpa looked towards the pool. The pool was filled with red blood. Grandpa moved towards the pool. His eyes started flowing. A sack in the middle of the pool floating.

Grandpa went down on his knees. He couldn't cry. He became speechless. He became motionless.

He stared at the sack in the pool without any distraction. He realised, he is now alone in this world, and he cried looking up to the sky 'please take me too.'

He noticed a piece of paper kept on the steps of the pool. The breeze made it move. Grandpa noticed the white paper. He moved towards the paper.

He took the paper with his hands and opened it.

Sir,

I am writing this letter, because you were a great inspiration for me and many other advocates. You are a great example of how an advocate should be.

I killed your son Dhamodhar, your grandson Reghu and his friend Johnson. I know what I have done is a crime, even if I have reasons to object.

I know, you already know the reason behind their murders. They ruined my family and life. They didn't listen to our pleas.

I lived my life till now, just to complete this mission and I never thought of the way I used to accomplish my mission. My advocate uncle, who saved our lives from them, who looked after my sister, who made me a lawyer and who told you all the stories.

I want you to know why they are dead, because no one deserves the pain of an unknown death in your family. That's why he told the entire story to you. Our Advocate uncle. Adv. Nandha Gopal, your Gopalji.

I am sorry for your loss. I am ready to take any punishment for what I have done.

Amaan Singh.

www.ingramcontent.com/pod-product-compliance
Lightning Source LLC
Chambersburg PA
CBHW020930160726
47993CB00005B/2209